GREEK MYTHOLOGY

THE ILIAD
THE TROJAN WAR

Stephanides Brothers'

GREEK MYTHOLOGY

THE ILIAD
THE TROJAN WAR

℞

Retold by Menelaos Stephanides
Drowings by Yannis Stephanides

Translation
Bruce Walter

SIGMA

THE ILIAD, THE TROJAN WAR

ISBN: 960-425-059-0
© 1997 Sigma Publications
Made and printed in Greece

20, Mavromihali St. tel.3607667 fax.3638941
GR-106 80 ATHENS GREECE

HELEN OF TROY: for three millennia her name
has conjured up a vision of loveliness glimpsed
through a nightmare of ruin and destruction.
'The face that launched a thousand ships' still
draws us with its fatal charm across the centuries, to live again the greatest tale of love and
war that man has ever told. For the Trojan War is
not some distant struggle seen hazily beyond the
gulf of time and myth, but a long campaign that
each of us fights in his heart, with the staunch
support of trusted comrades: a quest for beauty
lost and found again at last.

The translator

TABLE OF CONTENTS

BEFORE THE WAR

In that distant age when the earth was peopled by the mythical race of heroes, there stood on the eastern shore of the Aegean Sea a city ruled by king Priam – the fabled city of Troy. Yet for all its glory it was fated to endure a long and terrible war, brought on by the resentment of gods and men alike. Beneath its walls countless heroes were to fall in battle on both the Achaean and Trojan sides, until at last the mighty city was but smouldering ruins and all its brave defenders dead. And what was the cause of this great tragedy? The beauty of the king of Sparta's wife! But oh, what beauty that was – for none set eyes on the fair Helen who did not echo the words of the Trojan elders when they saw her in the tower above Troy's Scaean Gate: "The Achaeans are right to fight so many years over such a lovely creature; but then so are the Trojans!"

Who were the Achaeans — or the Trojans, for that matter?

The Achaeans were all those who lived in mainland Greece and were what are now called Greeks or Hellenes. Yet in those times they were not known by these names. The only ones whom Homer, the great poet of the Trojan war, referred to as 'Greeks' were Achilles and his Myrmidons. As for the others who fought alongside them, these he called 'Achaeans' or sometimes 'Argives' or 'Danaids' but never 'Greeks'.

And the Trojans? Perhaps they, too, were Greeks, like the Achaeans. Modern scholars tell us that they were, but then so does mythology. Indeed, so legend tells us, Troy was the favoured city of the great god of all the Hellenes, almighty Zeus; its walls were built by the two most truly Greek of all the gods, Apollo and Poseidon; while the sacred statue, the Palladium, which protected the city, was given to the Trojans by Athena herself. Indeed, the people of Troy not only shared in the worship of the gods of Olympus, but they spoke the same language as the other Greeks and had close relations with them. This was natural enough, for Troy lay on the Hellespont and in the same cradle of civilisation that had nurtured all the Greeks: the Aegean basin. However, in this war the Trojans' many allies included not only near but distant neighbours, people from the Asian hinterland who spoke outlandish tongues and were called 'barbarians' by the Greeks. Thus it has come to be remembered as a conflict between Greeks and

Trojans, as if the latter were some foreign race.

At this point it is worth seeing what Greek mythology has to tell us about the history of Troy. Curious as it may seem, the city's story begins in Crete. At some time in the distant past, that great island was stricken by drought. For two whole years there was no rain and the island's people were ravaged by famine. Eventually many of the Cretans took to their ships, determined to seek a new homeland. Led by Scamander, the son of Oceanus, they reached the entrance of the Hellespont and were enchanted by the beauty and lush greenery of those eastern shores.

"Here we shall make a fresh start", Scamander declared. "On this spot we shall build our homes and raise altars to our gods. All ashore now, first to make sacrifice to our saviour Zeus and then to work!"

A third of the people of Crete had left for this new land. Scamander, who became the first of their kings, remained for ever in the hearts of his subjects, not only because he had saved them but because when he died, being a son of Oceanus, he became a river-god and blessed the soil of his new homeland with bountiful supplies of water, so that his people would never again know the fear of drought and famine. From the start, this new river-god had two names: to the other gods he was known as Xanthus, but to his own people he remained for ever Scamander.

Thus the Trojans came from Crete – or so this legend tells us. Certainly the Cretan names which have survived in this region, such as the river Scamander and mount Ida, to name but two, bear witness that there is more than a grain of truth in the story. Besides, what would be more natural than for a great naval power, such as Crete was in those days, to have colonised the region which lies beside the straits leading to the Propontis and the Euxine Sea?

Yet the Athenians, too, could lay some ancient claims on Troy. They said that Teucer, one of its first kings, was an Athenian who hailed from the ancient deme of Troe, in Attica.

Whatever the truth of these conflicting claims, the founder of the line which gave Troy all its subsequent kings, right up to Priam, who was the last to rule, was neither Cretan nor Athenian. His name was Dardanus and he was said either to have come from Arcadia, in southern Greece, or even to have been born in Troy itself.

Dardanus was no ordinary mortal. His mother was Electra, Atlas' daughter, and his father none other than Zeus himself. Dardanus built a powerful state, Dardania, which subjected all the neighbouring peoples of Europe and Asia to its rule. Its capital was sited on the straits which have borne its founder's name from that time since: the Dardanelles. The name Hellespont was not given to the narrows until later, when Phrixus' sister Helle fell there and was drowned.

Dardanus had originally chosen another site on which to build his city, the hill where his descendants later founded Troy. However, he was warned by an oracle of Apollo that terrible misfortunes would befall the dwellers of any city which was built in that location. For it was on that very hill that Ate, goddess of deceit, had fallen when Zeus cast her out of Olympus.

Troy, which was also known as Ilium, was built by Ilus, son of Tros and grandson of Dardanus, but under the strangest circumstances.

Once Ilus was competing in the games in Phrygia. He won the victor's laurels in all the events and the king of Phrygia was so filled with admiration that he awarded him fifty young men and fifty maidens as a prize. On top of this he gave him a dappled cow, saying:

"Follow this beast, for it is sacred and will lead you to a site on which you must build a city of your own."

Pleased with his gifts, Ilus took the fifty youths and maidens and followed the holy animal. After first wandering aimlessly from place to place, it came at last to the hill of Ate, staggered to its summit and there, exhausted, sank upon the ground, thus indicating that on this spot the new city should be built.

Ilus stood there in consternation. What was he to do? Build on the same site that Dardanus had chosen for his capital, until Apollo's oracle had warned him off? Or should he ignore the choice made by the sacred cow and look for another place to build?

The decision was by no means easy. The oracle had said: "Those who live within the walls of the city built upon the hill of Ate will suffer terrible misfortunes." The warning seemed clear enough, but Ilus turned the words over and over in his mind. "Perhaps I haven't understood their true meaning," he kept telling himself. Finally he began to wonder exactly what was meant by the phrase 'who live within the walls of the city'. Then the answer came to him like a flash. "There are cities without walls," he told himself, "and without walls I shall build my city. Let Athena, who watches over the dwellings of men, be its guardian." With these words he called upon his fifty youths and maidens to begin the task immediately. But first of all he offered a sacrifice to the goddess. Then, having washed his arms, he raised them to the heavens and cried, "Watch over us, daughter of Zeus, and we shall build you a shining temple to honour and give praise to you for ever."

Soon work on the foundations was begun. It was Ilus who lifted high a pick and struck the first blow into the ground. And then, how strange! As he lifted out the first spadeful of earth a wooden statue was laid bare. It represented a young woman holding a spear in her right hand and a distaff in her left. Ilus understood. The goddess had heard his plea.

Though the new city would have no walls, it need not fear for anything. Nevertheless, Ilus consulted the oracle to learn more about his find. Finally he learned that the wooden statue was the Palladium. It had been made by Athena herself in memory of Pallas, her inseparable friend, who had died in the flower of her youth when the goddess made a careless throw with her lance in a war game. So that she would never forget her dear friend's face and form, the goddess had carved this wooden statue, and to be certain that Pallas would remain forever fresh in her memory she had placed her name beside her own – and had from that day on been known as Pallas Athena. More important still,

...the holy animal, exhausted, sank upon the ground, thus indicating that on this spot the new city should be built...

Ilus learned from the oracle that the goddess had agreed to watch over the new city – under one condition: the Palladium must never be lost. "If it is," the oracle declared, "then the whole city will disappear along with it."

The new city quickly rose, and to honour his father Tros, Ilus called it Troy. However, since Ilus had been its builder, the city was also known as Ilium. It became a fair city, with wide streets and gracious buildings. High on the acropolis Ilus built his palace and on its very summit the splendid temple of Athena containing the Palladium, the statue which guarded the unwalled city.

After the building of Troy the country was divided into two parts, Ilus ruling over Troy itself, while his brother Assaracus became king of neighbouring Dardanus.

On Ilus' death his son Laomedon assumed the throne of Troy. Zeus showed great favour to the young king, and it was on his orders that Apollo and Poseidon built the city's towering and impregnable walls. But Laomedon was anything but grateful for the love which the great ruler of gods and men had shown towards him, and for all Apollo and Poseidon's help he cheated them of their wages. He paid a heavy price for his meanness, however, and in the end his ingratitude cost him his life. He was killed by Heracles when the latter conquered Troy, because he showed himself equally ungrateful when the hero saved his daughter Hesione from a hideous and certain death. All this, however, can be found in greater detail in the volume in this series on Heracles, which also tells how, after Laomedon's death, his son Podarces became king of Troy and took the name of Priam. Podarces, who had been captured by Heracles, owed his freedom to his sister Hesione and the throne of Troy to the great hero's generosity. Before leaving for Salamis, where she was to be married to Telamon, Hesione begged Heracles to free her brother, and in exchange offered him the only thing she had left to give – her veil. Touched by her gesture, Heracles not only freed Podarces but made him king of Troy, giving him the name Priam, which means 'he who has been ransomed'. The young king was never to forget the debt he owed to his sister.

Priam, the last, tragic king of Troy, ruled for many years and was an old man by the time the war broke out. He had a great number of children – fifty sons and twelve daughters. Nineteen of these sons he had by his wife, Hecabe. Her first-born was Hector, the greatest of the Trojan generals. Her second son was the handsome and well-built Paris, of whom, however, for all his qualities his parents were often to say, "Better he had not been born" – for it was because of Paris that Troy fell.

The story of Paris begins in a dramatic way and ends in even greater drama. The day before his birth, his mother Hecabe dreamt that a great fire had engulfed the whole of Troy. She woke in terror and told her husband of the dream. He in turn consulted the oracle and was told that the child about to come into the world would be the cause of a fearsome war and that if they wanted their city to be saved the infant must be sacrificed.

Hecabe would not even hear of such a thing, but Priam was determined to protect his people and so he gave the new-born child to his herdsman Agelaus to be killed. He, however, was too soft-hearted even to hurt a fly, let alone slay an innocent little baby prince, and so he left him unharmed in the forest on the slopes of mount Ida. Yet even this troubled his conscience so much that he could not find a moment's rest. Terrified that the infant might be torn apart by wild beasts, he returned to the woods where he found it being suckled by a bear. Filled with joy and relief at the sight, and telling himself this was a sign that the gods wished the child to live, he took it home to his hut to be brought up with his own son who had been born a few days earlier.

Agelaus and his wife grew to love the king's son even more than their own child. As for giving him a name, it happened almost by itself.

"Keep an eye on the basket," the herdsman would tell his wife each time he went off with his flocks, for that was where they kept the child that they had saved.

"Mind the basket," Agelaus' wife would warn him whenever he returned. That basket was always uppermost in their minds. And since the word for basket in those days was 'paris', this was the name the little boy grew up with.

Paris' noble blood soon showed in his outstanding grace, intelligence and strength. While he was still little more than a child, a herd of oxen was stolen from Agelaus. Paris tracked down the rustlers and recovered the missing animals. From then on he was given the name Alexander, which means 'valiant defender'.

Paris grew up believing himself to be the son of Agelaus. He, too, became a herdsman and wandered with his flocks over the foothills of mount Ida. He was loved for his beauty by a nymph, Oenone, and together they spent happy hours splashing in the cool mountain streams or sitting under the shade of the overhanging plane-trees. For Paris, their union was just a carefree friendship, but for Oenone it was something much deeper. She knew, however, that Paris would not remain for ever at her side and this gave her double pain — not only that she would lose him, but that when she did so he might suffer great misfortune.

"May you always be carefree and happy — but if ever you are wounded, come to me — for I alone can cure your ills," Oonone told him, for she could see into the future.

But Paris, who did not yet know what pain and suffering were, could not understand the words of the far-seeing nymph. And so he passed his days untroubled, sometimes in the company of the lovely Oenone, sometimes with his herd and sometimes — this was a favourite sport of his — setting his bulls to fight among each other. From these bullfights Paris soon singled out a bull which always beat the rest. He gave it his special care and loved it more than any other in his herd.

One day, while he was grazing his animals on the highest slopes of mount Ida, still thinking he was nothing but a common herdsman, three goddesses and a god suddenly appeared before him. They were Hera, Athena, Aphrodite and wing-heeled Hermes.

Why had these four immortals come to Paris, and what did they want of him? To find the answer to that question we must go back several years in time and to the opposite shore of the Aegean, to tree-covered Pelion where the wedding was being celebrated between the sea-goddess Thetis and the hero Peleus, the son of Aeacus.

How Peleus came to marry Thetis is a story we have already told in another volume. Here we shall tell of the wedding-feast itself, where the first seeds of the terrible war of Troy were sown — for it was at this feast that Eris tossed down the famous golden apple.

The wedding took place outside the cave of the centaur Cheiron and all the gods attended it save Eris. Zeus himself had been against inviting her, lest this goddess, who loved strife and quarrels, should spoil the festivities.

As it was, everything got off to a happy start. The guests were in a cheerful mood and the atmosphere was warm and friendly. Apollo himself began the merrymaking with a sweep of his fingers across his golden lyre. The Muses hymned the new couple in their matchless voices and the three Fates sang to prophesy the glory of the hero who was destined to be born of this union — none other than the mighty Achilles.

The next morning, all those who had been invited passed before the 'epaulis', as in those days they called the hut of branches set up in a meadow where the newly-weds were accustomed to spend the first night of their marriage. The epaulis of Peleus and Thetis was no mean hut, however, but a miniature palace which Hephaestus himself had built the couple as a special favour. Here the gods left their presents. Some of these were truly beyond price, such as Poseidon's gift, the two immortal horses, Valius and Xanthus, which had the power of human speech, or the golden armour, the gift of all the gods, or the famous lance given by Cheiron, so heavy that none but Peleus could wield it, but which his son Achilles would later be able to handle with consummate ease.

The ceremonies were drawing to a successful conclusion and Hera, Athena and Aphrodite were engaged in friendly conversation, when over them, invisible, swept Eris. Resentful at not having been invited to the wedding, she tossed an apple at their feet. The goddesses looked down in surprise and Peleus, who was standing near, bent down and picked it up

"There are three words written on it," he said: 'To the fairest'.

"Then it must be for me," was Hera's immediate response.

"No, it's mine," Athena retorted curtly.

"Yes, but I'm the most beautiful," said Aphrodite in her coquettish voice.

Immediately a quarrel broke out among the three goddesses, with each of them claiming that she was the fairest of all and that the apple was for her.

So the wedding ended with bitter words, and worse still the goddesses were now sworn enemies. Years passed, but their resentment smouldered on. Finally Zeus could no

longer bear to see the three like this and ordered Hermes to
take Eris' apple and lead them to the summit of mount Ida
where Paris would decide which of the trio should have the
apple and thus, Zeus hoped, effect a reconciliation.

But why Paris? Why this obscure herdsman – even if he
was the son of Priam?

That was exactly why. The cruel Fates had decided everything in advance. The jealousy of the three goddesses was
predestined to lead them to this point: to bring the Achaeans evil fortune and utter destruction down upon the Trojans.

Surprise and terror seized Paris when he beheld Hermes
with the three goddesses. He was about to take to his heels
but Hermes pulled him gently back.

"Do not be afraid," he told him. "We have not come here
to do you any harm. On the contrary, Almighty Zeus, ruler
of gods and men, has decided to do you a great honour, for
he admires both your good looks and your judgement. Take
this apple. Great Zeus commands you to give it to the
fairest of the three."

"I, a humble shepherd, to sit in judgement on three immortals and decree which is the loveliest? No, I'd rather cut
the apple in three; it's the only way I can avoid doing an
injustice to any of them. Each is a goddess of Olympus and
lovelier than any woman on this earth."

"Yet each considers herself fairer than the other two and
it is the will of Zeus that you should resolve their quarrel.
He has no wish to be involved himself and nor has any
other god."

Thus Paris was obliged to sit in judgement on the three great goddesses. However, he preferred to examine them one by one. First he called Hera to him. The great lady of Olympus approached with stately step.

"Look at me carefully," she commanded, and turning slowly she revealed to Paris all her heavenly charms. "And remember," she told him as she turned again to leave, "if you decide wisely and give me the apple, I shall make you ruler of all Asia and the richest man on earth."

"I am sorry, but I am not to be bought," replied Paris, without stopping to think how much this would offend the goddess. "However, I thank you all the same. Now I shall see the daughter of Zeus."

Athena advanced towards him with steady confidence. Her burnished helmet glittered in the sun.

"You are an intelligent man," she told him. "Look at me and judge. But first hear what I have to tell you. If you give me the prize, I shall make you not only the mightiest warrior but the wisest man on earth."

"I am a mere shepherd and I love neither war nor fighting. The kingdom of Priam is a powerful one and peace is assured in his realms," replied Paris, offending Athena as much as he had done Hera. "As for the apple," he added, "I shall not treat you unjustly if you deserve to win it."

Finally Aphrodite ran towards him with a winning smile upon her lips.

"Look how beautiful I am!" she cried with a graceful gesture. "But then what about yourself? As soon as I set eyes on you, I knew there couldn't be a handsomer young man on earth. Surely, if anyone deserves good fortune you are he. So, listen to me. I have a partner waiting for you, a queen who is as beautiful as me. If she as much as looks upon your face, I am sure she will leave her family, her palace, and everything in the world, just to be yours. It is fair Helen whom I speak of. You must have heard of her divine loveliness?"

"I never so much as heard her name till now. But please, tell me more about her."

"Her mother is the beauteous Leda, daughter of the king of Aetolia, and her father a snow-white swan who was none other than Zeus himself. She was scarcely a girl when war broke out between Sparta and Athens over her beauty. All the young princes of Greece longed to have her for a wife but she took Menelaus, king of Sparta as her husband. However, if you want, I will help her to become yours."

"But that's impossible. She's married already — and to a king at that!"

"Oh, father Zeus! What a child we have here! Don't you know what my business is? Have you never heard that it is among my divine duties to resolve problems of the heart? Listen to me. While I am at your side you shall have whatever your soul desires. I am the goddess of love — I suppose you understand what that means? Give me my due and hand the apple over."

Paris understood. It meant this humble shepherd could take for his wife the daughter of Zeus, the loveliest creature ever born into the world. It was beyond belief — and yet it could be done.

...So Paris gave the apple to Aphrodite...

"I do not have the strength to resist what you propose," he told the goddess. "My heart desires fair Helen already!"

"You shall have her, that I swear!" replied the goddess.

So Paris gave the apple to Aphrodite.

That was all that was needed; the two other goddesses swore revenge: a terrible fate would befall the whole of Troy.

It was not many days after this that some of Priam's soldiers came to mount Ida to choose a bull. They wanted the beast as a prize in the games which were about to be held in memory of the king of Troy's son, who, of course, was none other than Paris, for everyone believed him dead. But the bull they chose was the very one that Paris loved so dearly, and rather than be separated from it, the young herdsman decided to accompany the soldiers to Troy so he could take part in the contests and win his treasured champion back.

"A shepherd boy competing in the games?" cried Agelaus as soon as he heard of this. "No, such events are not for the likes of you!"

But Paris was determined to win back his bull. Besides, he was no longer a mere herdsman. Was he not to marry the lovely Helen, daughter of Zeus? And did not the victor's prize belong to him by right? So when the games started, he was there.

Boldly stepping out before the royal throne, he took on the finest wrestler in Troy. More by courage than by skill he managed to defeat him. Next he took part in the running event and came first, leaving behind him Priam's fleetest sons. Those that had lost to him felt themselves insulted and challenged him to another contest. Yet again he beat them. Three defeats at the hands of a mere herd boy – this was more than the king's sons could endure. They angrily cried out he had beaten them by some trickery and one of them, Deiphobus, lunged for the kill. But Paris nimbly evaded him and leapt up on the altar of Zeus, while Agelaus ran to Priam and Hecabe, crying:

"What are you trying to do? This young man is none other than he whose memory you are honouring today! Forgive me, but I could not find it in my heart to carry out your order all those years ago. I could not kill your son when you gave him as a babe into my hands."

"And how can you prove the truth of what you say?"

"This baby's rattle is proof enough, I think."

As soon as she saw it, Hecabe wept tears of joy. Her husband was as pleased as she. But when the priests of Apollo heard the news, they hastened to Priam and reminded him of the old oracle:

"Paris must die, or Troy will be destroyed."

But Priam would not agree to this.

"I would rather all Troy were reduced to ashes than lose this wonderful son of mine!" he shouted.

So Paris was accepted by Priam and his brothers. They even suggested he should marry, but he dreamt of none but the fair Helen, daughter of the white swan.

Then one day, quite unexpectedly, Helen's husband Menelaus arrived in Troy. He had come in obedience to the command of the oracle at Delphi: he was to find and bring home the bones of two Spartans who had been killed at Troy during Heracles' conquest of the city. Paris himself arranged for Menelaus' accommodation and helped him to find the remains of the two heroes. It was a unique opportunity to get to know his rival, and he made good use of it. On his departure, Menelaus thanked Paris with all his heart:

"Only if you come to Sparta one day will I be able to repay the help and hospitality you have given me so willingly," he told him.

This was just what Paris had been hoping for.

"I will move heaven and earth to make a visit possible," he assured him.

Thus Menelaus left Troy with the happiest of memories, not guessing for a moment why Paris should want to come and visit him in Sparta.

Shortly after this, Priam decided to send envoys to Salamis. He wished to ask for the return of his sister Hesione, whom Telamon had taken when he and Heracles had invaded Troy. Hesione would be an old woman by now and Priam wished to have her with him once again, so he asked who would be willing to go to Salamis.

Paris offered his services with alacrity.

"And if they will not give her to me," he added, "I will find some other princess, kidnap her and bring her back to Troy as a bargaining tool for Hesione."

Of course, no one saw anything suspicious in his words and a fine, swift vessel was got ready for the voyage. Priam sent rich gifts for the king of Salamis, while Paris chose the crew himself. Among them was his cousin Aeneas, the son of Aphrodite.

The day of their departure came. A lot of well-wishers had come down to the port to see the ship off. Then suddenly, while Paris was receiving his farewells, a cry was heard.

"Don't let Paris sail! This voyage will bring ruin upon Troy!" It was Cassandra, Paris' sister, who had shouted. But nobody believed her, any more than they believed the rest of her true prophesies. The voyage would take place. The fall of Troy was now a certainty.

Shortly before Paris went on board, a girl dashed out from among the crowd and flung herself into his arms. It was his friend Oenone, the nymph of the forests. Her magic powers had sensed the disaster that was destined to befall the Trojans, but she knew that it would serve no purpose to speak of it. All she did was to say once more:

"If ever you are wounded, come to me – for only I can cure your ills."

Paris answered her with a parting kiss and a tear which trickled down his cheek. But the tear soon dried and his thoughts swiftly returned to fair Helen and adventure. When he next remembered Oenone it was already much too late.

The ship left harbour. Borne along on a favouring wind sent by Aphrodite it soon arrived – not, of course, at Salamis but on the shores of Sparta.

Taking the gifts entrusted to him by his father, Paris set off with his companions for the city and the palace of

Menelaus.

Before leaving Troy, Paris had taken the trouble to learn as much as he could about Helen. However, he failed to discover the most important fact of all — and had he done so he might never have undertaken the voyage. But let us begin the story of fair Helen from the beginning.

Before Menelaus, Sparta was governed by Tyndareos. He loved the beautiful Leda, daughter of Thestius. This king of Pleuron had two girls, both as lovely as goddesses. The elder of them, Althaea, married Oeneus of Calydon and bore him the renowned hero Meleager. Leda, the younger, was wedded to Tyndareos. When her time came to give birth something happened which was beyond all belief. First she bore a daughter and then... laid two eggs! Filled with amazement, Tyndareos hastened to consult the oracle — and the answer given him by Apollo's priests was this:

"Leda, the beautiful princess you married, has not been loved by you alone but by the ruler of gods and men as well, great Zeus, who came down on her transformed into a swan. That is why your wife laid the two eggs. From one of them will hatch a daughter who will become the loveliest woman in the world and from the other two boys who will grow into great heroes. You must love and care for the children entrusted to you by almighty Zeus with even greater love than you give to your own daughter. And you must exercise particular judgement when the time comes for you to give away Zeus' female child in marriage, for we

...Zeus came down on her transformed into a swan...

foresee that on account of her great beauty a long and terrible war will be waged."

This daughter, of course, was none other than the fair Helen. The two boys were Castor and Polydeuces, who were also known as the Twins because they had been hatched from the same egg and the Dioscuri because they were 'kouroi' or sons of Zeus. The daughter who was born before their mother laid the eggs was Clytemnestra, whom Tyndareos had fathered.

Helen was Zeus' only daughter by a mortal woman, and her unimaginable beauty was talked of in the furthest corners of the earth. She was scarcely twelve years old when Theseus saw her and fell madly in love. He secretly snatched her away from her father's house, causing a war to erupt between Sparta and Athens. Later, when she grew into the first bloom of womanhood and Tyndareos decided to find a husband for her, there was not a young prince in all Greece who did not come to Sparta bearing rich gifts, to seek her hand in marriage. This troubled Tyndareos, who feared that the old oracle of the priests of Apollo, warning of a fearsome war, might now prove true. "A thousand times better to have had a daughter that no one found attractive," Tyndareos often told himself, "rather than this Helen whose beauty looks as if it's going to set the world on fire." Because of this he did not settle on any of the suitors and nor did he accept a single gift for fear that what pleased one might give offence to all the rest. However, he was rescued from this awkward situation by the crafty Odysseus, king of Ithaca.

Odysseus had come to Sparta with the other suitors, yet he had no great desire to win Helen's hand and thus he had brought no gift along. "Helen will fall to Menelaus," he reasoned. "He's the richest and most handsome — and besides, who can stand against him when he has the support of his brother Agamemnon, the great king of Mycenae? He will be the lucky one — but if he really proves to be a winner, only time will tell." Besides, Odysseus knew that of all the young princes competing for her favours, Menelaus was the one whom Helen preferred.

"I don't know how you're going to take this," he told Tyndareos, "but I didn't come here for your daughter. To tell you the truth, I've no great wish to be yoked to the world's most beautiful woman."

"And you thought that would offend me? I've always respected intelligent men, and you're behaving a good deal more sensibly than all the others. If I seem indecisive to you it is because an oracle has warned me that Helen's beauty could prove the cause of a long and terrible war. Quite honestly, I am afraid."

"I would be, too — oracle or no oracle. That's why you won't find me queuing to beg your lovely daughter's hand!"

"Then why did you come to Sparta?"

"For two reasons: first of all to ask you to do whatever lies within your power to help me win Penelope, the daughter of your brother Icarius; and secondly to aid you all I can in finding a solution to this problem which torments you. All I ask is that you promise to use all your influence on my behalf."

"I give you my word," was Tyndareos' immediate reply, and they shook hands on it.

"Listen, now," Odysseus continued. "Here is how it must be done. We shall make them all swear a solemn oath that whoever marries Helen, the others will come to his defence, even to the point of war, if any man ever dares to take her from him. And to avoid any personal enmity falling upon you, tell your daughter to choose her husband for herself."

Tyndareos was impressed by the wisdom of Odysseus' words and immediately announced them to the suitors, who had no alternative but to agree. A horse was sacrificed and butchered and they all stood round resting their right hands on the bleeding flesh while they repeated word for word the oath which Odysseus dictated to them. In the end, as the clever king of Ithaca had foreseen, Helen chose the hand-some, fair-haired Menelaus.

On marrying Helen, Menelaus became king of Sparta. There followed several years of tranquil married bliss with his lovely wife. A daughter, Hermione, was born to them and Menelaus was the happiest of men – until, one morning, two foreign messengers arrived.

"Most honoured and worthy king of heroic Sparta," said one of them, "we come from fabled Ilium. In our footsteps there follows, on a friendly visit, the glorious Alexander, Paris, son of the king of Troy! He is returning the visit which you once paid him when duty brought you to the city of Priam."

Menelaus could hardly contain himself for joy. He immediately called for his wife and told her the happy news. She put on her finest robes and adorned herself with jewels, then they all walked down to the entrance of the palace to welcome the young prince of Troy.

In a short while they could make out the visitors approaching along the road. Zeus' daughter stood at Menelaus' side filled with joy and secret pride: for not only was she blessed with divine good looks but so, too, was her husband. Menelaus was truly the fairest and the best-built man of all the rulers of Greece. But when their guests drew nearer and Helen's eyes met the gaze of the divinely handsome Paris, her heart was transfixed by a burning shaft of love. Aphrodite's winged son Eros had pierced her with his arrow. One look from Paris and she was enslaved. Her attractive, fair- haired husband might never have existed.

Paris, too, was in a tumult of bewitchment. Was this a divine vision which his eyes beheld? "I have found the beauty of all my dreams," he told himself. It seemed incredible, but when he remembered the goddess Aphrodite's promise he gave free rein to his thoughts. "And yet she shall be mine," he said and moved forward with a firm step to greet her. Then he was welcomed by the delighted Menelaus, who invited his visitors to walk up to the palace. The king of Sparta was deeply touched by the splendid gifts which Paris presented to him and to his wife. At the dinner table he placed him in the seat of honour on his right hand, between himself and Helen. Aeneas he seated on his left and was soon deep in conversation with him, while

Paris and Helen, caught in the toils of love, murmured sweet words of endearment.

The next day, Paris found Helen sitting by herself. "Listen," he said. "It is for you alone that I have made this voyage. I have come to take you away. Aphrodite has planted in my heart a flower of desire which can never be uprooted. But it is not the goddess of love alone who wills that this be so. Almighty Zeus decreed it first, when he chose me to judge which of the three goddesses, Hera, Athena or Aphrodite was the fairest. I gave the prize to Aphrodite and she promised me the loveliest woman in the world. 'Helen is her name,' she told me, 'and she is the daughter of Zeus.' I made up my mind and brushed all obstacles aside. It is for your sake only that I have crossed the broad seas. Do not deny my love. Come, let us leave for Troy."

Paris' proposal was more than Helen could resist. The fire which Aphrodite had kindled in her heart made her incapable of all thought of her loving husband, of the daughter she longed to have always at her side and of all her people, who both admired and respected her.

"I know that what I am about to do is wrong," she said, "but it is beyond my powers to do otherwise. I fell under a spell the moment I set eyes on you. One moment I thought Apollo stood before me, the next it was Dionysus and then Eros himself. The wrath of Menelaus troubles me but little now, for you and mighty Ilium will protect me."

Meanwhile Menelaus, who was naturally kind-hearted and hospitable, continued to entertain his guests for nine

...The couple slipped in the depths of night...

whole days, never once suspecting that Paris might be plotting to run off with his wife. And when their opportunity did come, it was Menelaus himself who gave it. On the tenth day he sailed for Crete, to be present at the burial of his grandfather, who had died unexpectedly. Before leaving, he told Helen:

"You must look after our guests while I am away. Make sure that they lack for nothing. I leave you in my place and trust you to take care of them as if I were here in person."

Helen gave her word that everything would be carried out according to his instructions, but as soon as her husband had sailed away she began to make preparations for the fateful voyage.

The couple slipped out of the palace in the depths of night. Helen took with her her two most faithful slaves and everything she possessed, including clothes and jewellery. But as if to ensure that the horrors of war would descend upon them all, some madness put it in their minds to rob Menelaus' treasure-vaults. They left them standing empty. It seemed as if the gods had indeed willed Troy's destruction.

Hastily they made their way down to the sea and set sail for Cranae, a small island off the coast of modern Gytheion. There the two lovers spent their first night together, and ever since it has been called Fair Helen's Island. From here on, though, their voyage was by no means easy. Contrary winds drove their ship towards Cyprus. Even when the weather mended, Paris preferred to wander far off course, dropping anchor in Egypt and

Phoenicia for fear that Menelaus might be in pursuit further north. Only months later did they reach Troy, when Paris was satisfied there would be no unwelcome encounter along their route.

Menelaus' rage when he returned to Sparta was terrible to behold.

"We must prepare for war!" he roared and galloped off to Mycenae to find his brother.

Agamemnon agreed to it at once, and the two brothers decided to call on all those who had sworn the oath upon the butchered horse. But first they went to seek the counsel of Nestor of Pylos, the oldest and wisest of all the kings of Greece. He, too, agreed that war must be declared and even offered to go with them to help raise not only those cities whose rulers had given their word, but others who had not been at the gathering of Helen's suitors. They set off to gather forces to their side.

"Paris and his people must be punished harshly," Menelaus insisted. "It's the only way to ensure that no one else ever dares to snatch our wives away and rob us of our wealth."

Many who heard were willing to take part. Others were more hesitant.

"It's only once in a thousand years a king has his wife stolen from him," they replied. "You are interested in getting back your wife, and we understand that. But what gain is there for us in this affair?"

Menelaus' answer silenced all their doubts.

"Troy is a prosperous city. The treasuries of Priam hold

wealth beyond imagining and yet you still ask me what gain this venture holds for you. Do you not yet understand?"

However, there was one ruler who had no desire whatsoever to take part in this campaign. He was the one who had made the suitors swear upon the butchered horse – Odysseus of Ithaca.

Odysseus was not only the most intelligent but also the sharpest of the Achaean leaders. Indeed, he was so notorious for his crafty tricks that many people believed his father was not Laertes, as was officially given out, but Sisyphus, who had been sly enough to fool the gods themselves.

This king of Ithaca had not been attracted for an instant by the idea of marrying the loveliest creature in the world, remember. He had set his sights on Penelope, the daughter of Icarius, even though she could not hold a candle to Helen as far as good looks went. But whatever looks she had were more than enough for Odysseus, who considered it foolish to look on outward beauty alone. Other qualities had more value as far as he was concerned. If Penelope once became his, he was quite sure his she would remain – for ever. As events turned out, he was quite right. However, actually winning her hand turned out to be no easy matter and he only accomplished it thanks to his own cunning and the help of Tyndareos, who faithfully kept the promise he had given. So it was that in the games Icarius held to find a champion worthy of his daughter, it was Tyndareos who excused and covered up all Odysseus' crafty tricks and cheating.

For all this, Icarius saw exactly what was going on and was determined to exclude him.

"Now don't be such a fool," Tyndareos told his brother. "Odysseus has beaten everyone in the game that matters most: the game of wits!"

So in the end Icarius was persuaded. But so deeply did he love his daughter that he could not bear the thought of separation from her.

"Come and live with us," he told Odysseus, "and when I die, my throne shall be yours."

"My homeland is Ithaca," replied Odysseus, "and that is throne enough for me. Penelope must come back to my island."

Icarius, however, continued to insist till in the end Odysseus lost all patience, seized Penelope, jumped into his chariot, whipped up the horses and set off at a gallop for Ithaca. A little north of Sparta, Icarius caught up with them.

"Listen, Penelope," Odysseus said at last, "either you come with me or you stay with your father. It's up to you."

But Penelope could not make up her mind. She had been brought up to obey her father. She loved Odysseus but was ashamed to admit that she wanted to go away with him. All she could do now was pull her veil down over her face and remain silent. Then her father, moved by her gesture and seeing that Odysseus was in the right, decided to let her go with him. Later, in appreciation of his daughter's conduct, he raised a statue of Humility in the place where this had happened.

So Odysseus married the woman he had chosen with his heart and with his mind. He had been ruling happily on Ithaca for some years and had even acquired a delightful little son, Telemachus, when the news came that Paris had eloped with Helen.

"Things look bad," he told Penelope. "Menelaus and Agamemnon seem set to raise the whole of Greece. They'll be coming for me soon, just wait and see. Everyone knows they can't launch an expedition against Troy without Odysseus' brains behind it; but I'm blessed if I want to ruin our happiness by running off to fight in foreign parts. They could hand me all Priam's treasure on a plate and I'd still say no. Besides, Menelaus wanted that Helen woman, so let him pay for his own mistakes. What's it got to do with me? And what have you done to deserve being separated from your husband, the father of your child, and live from day to day not knowing if he'll ever return? What has Greece done to deserve all this, for that matter? Is it our fault if Menelaus kept a young demigod like Paris wined and dined in his house for nine whole days and nights – and then, when the fellow's got to leave for Crete, instead of taking Paris by the arm and saying, 'I'll just come down to the harbour to see you off', he goes and leaves him alone in his own house, to be looked after by Helen of all people! Why, the man's as stupid as they come. I'm not saying he's not brave, mind you but as for having what it takes up here, it's clear that he hasn't got too much between his ears! I'll tell you what I'll do, though: here on Ithaca we've got a good soothsayer, Alitherses is his name. I'll ask him what my

...The news soon spread throughout Greece that Odysseus
had lost his mind...

chances would be if I went over to Troy. If it looks like being a short trip, then I'll go — but if he tells me things look black for old Odysseus, then I'll have to find a way to wriggle out of this one. After all, it was the others swore the oath, not me."

Alitherses prophesied Odysseus' future — and he prophesied correctly.

"If you leave for Troy," he said, "you will return unrecognisable, after twenty whole years have gone by, and all your companions have been lost!"

That was enough for Odysseus. "I'll pretend I have gone mad," he decided, "and then I won't have to go to Troy!"

The news soon spread throughout Greece that Odysseus had lost his mind. But Palamedes, son of Nauplius, a man as intelligent as Odysseus himself, told Menelaus and Agamemnon:

"He's the last person in the world who would ever fall insane. Let's go and get him!"

The three leaders went to Ithaca and found Odysseus ploughing a field, with an ox and a donkey yoked to the shafts — and sowing salt behind him as he went. When his visitors approached, he pretended not to know them and went on scattering salt into the furrows. Penelope stood nearby, the babe in her arms, anxiously watching the three leaders. Suddenly, Palamedes snatched Telemachus from her breast and dropped the little boy right in the path of Odysseus' plough, crying, "Odysseus, come with us!" To avoid killing his own child, Odysseus heaved the plough to an abrupt halt and was forced to admit that he had put on this show of madness for a purpose. In the end he added:

"Anyway, let's forget about all that. Off we go to conquer Troy. When it comes to backing Menelaus, you'll find me second to no man!"

But as for Palamedes, Odysseus bore him a lasting grudge.

While all the other leaders and heroes of Greece had now come together, one of them was still nowhere to be found. This was Achilles, son of Thetis and Peleus, king of Phthia. His absence was very strange, since Achilles was perhaps the only one of them who would not gladly have avoided this war.

Achilles was a youth of fearsome strength. His mother Thetis, knowing in advance how strong her son was destined to become, wished to make him immortal as well. To achieve this, she dipped him in the waters of the subterranean river Styx while he was still a baby, and as a result his whole body became proof against weapons and sickness — all, that is, except the heel by which she had held him. Next she went to the wise centaur Cheiron, to have him brought up on mount Pelion and exercised in mind and body. Achilles' upbringing started with his diet: Cheiron fed him on bear's brain to make him intelligent, on venison to give him the swiftness of a deer and lions' hearts to give him the courage of the king of beasts. He trained him in chariot-racing, in hunting and above all in the arts of war. But alongside these Achilles was taught letters, astronomy and even medicine. The muse Calliope was summoned to reveal the magic world of music to him. Achilles was an intelligent child who learned things quickly. He became a strong, fleet-footed runner and loved hunting and the heavy spear. He could run deer down without the help of dogs and was only six years old when he killed his first bear. From then on, he often dragged the corpses not only of bears but lions to the mouth of Cheiron's cave. Finally the day came when the wise Centaur told him:

"You have learned more than I would ever have believed possible. From now on, let duty be your teacher."

When the news came that Paris had abducted Helen, Achilles was at his family home in Phthia. He was only fifteen years old by this time but had already been appointed general of the Phthian forces, the renowned Myrmidons, and was preparing for war before the scandal was even mentioned to him.

Meanwhile, his mother Thetis was being eaten away by grief, for she knew that her son would be killed in the flower of his youth, pursuing the Trojans. Apollo had told her clearly: "Achilles will escape death only if he does not go to Troy."

And so Thetis decided to hide Achilles away. She dressed him as a girl and sent him off to the palace of king Lycomedes, on the island of Scyros.

There Achilles lived with the daughters of the king, who called him Pyrrha because of his fiery red hair. But the soothsayer Calchas had foretold that Troy would never be taken without Achilles' aid and so the leaders of the expedition began to search. Finally they discovered that he was to be found at the palace of Lycomedes. On receiving this

...Thetis wished to make him immortal as well. To achieve this, she dipped him in the waters of the subterranean river Styx...

news, Odysseus chose a few companions and took ship for Scyros.

"There's no Achilles here, nor any boy for that matter," Lycomedes told them.

"Perhaps not, but will you let us search?" Odysseus requested.

"Search to your heart's content," was Lycomedes' reply.

They turned the palace inside out, but all they found was girls.

"That's all right, then," said Odysseus, "but before we leave we'd like to give your daughters a few presents for scaring them unnecessarily."

Going down to the ship, they brought up a pile of gifts of the sort that would appeal to young ladies – but among them were a shield and a spear. They laid the gifts out on a large table.

The girls began to rummage through the presents, but one of them, a maiden with hair as red as fire, showed no interest in choosing anything.

Suddenly a trumpet-blast was heard. War cries rang out, and the clash of arms, as if a battle were raging. It was Odysseus' men who were making all this racket, following the instructions that their chief had given them. In a flash, the red-haired girl seized the shield and the spear, which were all that was left on the table, and dashed outside.

Odysseus knew that this must be Achilles. He ran to stop him and told the young man who he was and the reason he had come. Achilles accompanied him gladly, tearing off his girl's clothes in disgust.

Before leaving Scyros, however, he went to bid farewell to the king and his daughters. One of them, the lovely Deidameia, could not hold back her tears. Deeply moved, Achilles said his last goodbyes to her. It was clear that there was some great secret between this pair.

From Scyros, Achilles returned to his homeland to prepare for war. He found a ready helper in his cousin Patroclus, son of Menoetius, king of Locris. Hounded from his father's home by a vendetta, he had found shelter under his uncle Peleus' roof. Though older than Achilles, Patroclus became his inseparable companion and often helped his cousin with his wise words and encouragement in times both of joy and sorrow.

With tears streaming down his cheeks, but filled with secret pride, old Peleus bade farewell to his son and handed him the most precious objects a warrior could possess: his magnificent weapons, the like of which the world had never known, for the gods themselves had presented them to him upon his marriage to Thetis. Among them were his famous heavy spear; then there were the two immortal talking horses, these too a wedding-gift from earth-shaker Poseidon, god of the oceans. He also gave his impulsive and inexperienced son a wonderful counsellor, the wise Phoenix, who was to prove to the young man as much a second father as a teacher. But besides all these, the son of Peleus had under his command the formidable army of the Myrmidons — and of course his brave friend Patroclus, who would be always at his side. Achilles seemed to be leaving for this war with invincible powers. Let us not forget that his whole body was proof against all weapons, except the part by which Thetis had held him in the Styx: the 'Achilles' heel', as the weak point in that which is otherwise strong has ever since been called.

Yet this hero was destined to be slain. He himself knew it, for his mother had revealed his fate to him in the hope that he would be afraid to go to war. Poor deluded woman! Did she not know her own son, the boy of whom Prometheus once said that had his father been a god as well, then Zeus himself would go in fear of him?

As it was, nothing could hold Achilles back. He quickly assembled his army, and together with Patroclus they boarded fifty ships and set course for Aulis.

There, in the straits of Euboea, all the leaders of the Greeks were gathering, each with his soldiers and his ships.

The commander-in-chief and ruler over all the royal leaders of the Greek forces was stern Agamemnon, king of golden Mycenae. His wife was Clytemnestra, the sister of fair Helen. Agamemnon, who had brought a hundred ships to Aulis, wielded power on earth comparable to that which Zeus enjoyed on Olympus. No one questioned this – yet, for all the sway he held, he was neither the worthiest nor most just of the rulers of the Achaeans. Quite the opposite, in fact; for Agamemnon was the son of Atreus, and the family of the Atreids was accursed. His grandfather Pelops had laid his curse on his sons Atreus and Thyestes because they had murdered their brother. Pursued, they found shelter at Mycenae in the court of the boastful and cowardly king Eurystheus, Heracles' tyrannical master. As soon as Eurystheus died a bitter struggle of ambitious wills broke out over the throne of Mycenae. A string of crimes and hideous revenge culminated in the murder of Atreus by Thyestes' son Aegisthus and of Thyestes by Atreus' son Agamemnon. The evil destiny which burdened the Atreids was to dog Agamemnon's children, Iphigeneia, Electra and Orestes, in their turn.

Yet this was the dynasty which gave Greece her high kings, the dynasty which still held the sceptre of Zeus that Hermes had presented to Pelops. From Pelops it had gone to Atreus and Thyestes, and from Thyestes it had passed on to Agamemnon. He now held Zeus' sceptre, so he was now high king. Even if he broke the law, it was no longer of the slightest consequence, since all believed that it was Zeus and the cruel Fates which determined the course of human actions. Yet whatever power the great Atreid wielded, and however brave he may have been, in this war he was to prove so selfish, grasping and stubborn as to do great harm to the Achaean cause.

Menelaus, his good-hearted younger brother, was a very different character under normal circumstances. But now he was consumed by hatred for Paris, and it was only due to his insistent pressure that the expedition against Troy, to which he contributed sixty ships, ever took place at all. A brave and skilled fighter, Menelaus took on Paris in single combat and defeated him. He even had the courage to challenge the mighty Hector, though he knew full well how far he was outclassed. Had his brother Agamemnon not

stepped in and stopped him, he would have gone to certain death.

Many other Achaean leaders were to distinguish themselves in this war, but the greatest burden of the fighting at the critical hour would be borne by Ajax of Salamis. There was no finer warrior on the Greek side, except Achilles. Ajax was a burly, broad shouldered man who stood a head taller than the other combatants. With his towering shield and great long spear he looked like a battle-chieftain from some age long past. And like them, he used stones to fight with, huge rocks which he hurled with stunning force upon the enemy. Ajax' father Telamon had been the one who once stormed Troy with Heracles and carried off Priam's sister Hesione. Ajax was not Hesione's son, however. He

harboured a deadly hatred for the Trojans and sent twelve
ships against Troy.

At his side there fought another Ajax, the son of Oileus,
king of Locris. This Locridan Ajax led forty ships to Troy.
Short and slightly-built he may have been, but he could run
faster than the wind and was lightning-quick with sword
and spear. When these two Ajaxes charged into battle, only
the gods could stand before them.

Yet there was one hero who did fight against the gods.
This was Diomedes, king of Argus, who had Athena
always at his side. He was so bold and strong that men
compared him with great Ajax; and when setbacks in the
fighting would put fear into the hearts of many Greeks, he
remained unshaken in his determination to go on fighting

till the final victory. Diomedes set out for Troy at the head of eighty ships.

In the end, a mighty army assembled under the command of Agamemnon. Twelve hundred ships from thirty different regions sailed into Aulis, near the straits of Chalcis, from whence they would set course for Troy.

The brave Trojans would defend their homeland doggedly, for ten long years. Yet despite their many allies their forces would prove no match for the sheer weight of numbers of the Achaeans. Their main defence would be the tall walls of the city, built by gods. If Troy succeeded in holding out so long it was also due in great part to their superb commander, Hector, son of Priam and Hecabe.

Hector was a noble and yet tragic figure. Homer himself, the author of the Iliad, dedicates his most inspired verses to him, verses which send their message to us down the centuries, rising above the horror of a savage and relentless war: the enemy, too, is a man who struggles and suffers, who loves his dear ones and gives his life's blood for his homeland. Indeed, for Homer, there are no enemies or friends, no Greeks and no barbarians; there are only Trojans and Achaeans, men against men.

Hector was blessed with all the finest qualities: strong, brave, fair in mind and body, there was none could match him in the arts of war. If anything befell Hector, all would be lost — and everybody knew it. He was the rock on which Troy founded all her hopes now that his father was too old to do anything but sit and follow the defence his son was leading. His fighting qualities were known and feared by his enemies, too. When the invincible Achilles withdrew offended from the battle, Hector pursued the Achaeans right down to their ships. And when hatred for the Trojans swelled once more within Achilles' heart and he threw himself back into the fight, Hector was the only one who stayed to face the formidable Greek champion, although he knew himself outclassed. Who would not cling to life in the face of certain death? Yet Hector's brave heart would not let him flee in shame, and so the Trojan's greatest hero showed himself worthy of his reputation by standing to meet his end in battle, pierced by the war-lance of his superhuman adversary. The name of brave and noble Hector would live on for ever among friend and foe alike.

Second in rank among the Trojan heroes was Aeneas, son of the goddess Aphrodite and Anchises, king of Dardanus. Aphrodite had fallen in love with Anchises against her will. Mighty Zeus had grown tired of hearing her boast that she had never loved a mortal man, while he himself had succumbed to the charms of many earthly women. And so he filled her with uncontrollable desire for Anchises, who was as handsome as a god. She went and sought him out herself, on the slopes of mount Ida, where he was grazing his flocks. She did not reveal her true identity, however, but told him:

"I am the daughter of the king of Phrygia. Hermes himself visited me in my sleep and told me that I must become your wife."

Carried away by her beauty, Anchises believed her

story, and with the consent of mighty Zeus and implacable Fate he slept with a goddess without knowing who she was.

Thus was born the Aeneas who accompanied Paris to Sparta to help him carry off fair Helen. Aeneas was a fearless warrior — and if Hector was Troy's battle-arm, it was he who was her soul, as Achilles himself admitted.

His immortal mother kept constant guard over him and he was among the few Trojan heroes who were spared in the great slaughter.

The tragic end of Troy had been prophesied by Priam's daughter Cassandra, but nobody believed her — and here is why.

The divinely beautiful Cassandra had become a seer because the god Apollo fell in love with her. He offered her prophetic powers if she promised to return his love. She gave her word, but when the time came she refused to keep it. Apollo was furious, but he hid his feelings and asked her to give him a kiss at least. Suspecting nothing, she offered him her lips, whereupon Apollo spat into her mouth in vengeance.

What the god had done did not make Priam's daughter lose the power to see into the future, but it did make her unable to persuade people that her prophesies were true, which was even worse. Indeed, Troy would have been saved if its citizens had paid more attention to her unfailingly accurate predictions.

The Achaeans sailed twice for Troy. The first expedition failed because the fleet mistakenly made landfall in another country. The cause of this was that Agamemnon believed the fittest man to guide the Greek ships safely and unerringly to Troy was young Achilles. The way he reasoned it, the goddess Thetis would never leave her son to the mercy of the waves and thus they would all reach Troy if he piloted the fleet.

What Agamemnon thought was one thing; what Thetis had in mind was quite another. She knew her son would meet his death if he reached Troy, and so the course she mapped out for him was anything but the one he should have followed. She sent him in another direction altogether, and the fleet made landfall in Mysia, a region ruled by Heracles' brave and mighty son Telephus.

When the Achaeans went ashore, they immediately began to loot and destroy, believing they had landed on Trojan territory. When Telephus saw the evil intentions of these uninvited strangers he fell on them with his whole army, putting them to flight and killing many. The situation changed when Achilles and Patroclus came charging to the fore. Telephus succeeded in wounding Patroclus in the arm — but it would have been better for him if his blow had fallen wide. With a roar of rage, Achilles himself lunged forward to cross swords with him. One look at this terrible warlord was enough to tell Telephus that here was a warrior even he would be no match for, so he took to his heels. And he would have got away had the god Dionysus not stopped him in his flight. Telephus had had this coming to him, for he had neglected to honour the god with festivals and wild revels. So it was that, as he ran, a branch sprouted from the ground before him and Telephus stumbled and fell. A moment later Achilles caught him up and plunged his spear deep into his leg. It was no minor wound, for it opened a wide gash that would never easily heal. As for Patroclus' arm, Achilles tended it himself, in the way that the wise centaur Cheiron had taught him.

Finally the Achaeans went back on board their ships, but while they were continuing their search for Troy a terrible storm broke on them, scattering all the fleet. Their courage drooping, and with a bitter taste of how uncertain the outcome of such an expedition might prove, they turned their prows towards home and in the end each leader returned to his own lands with his army. Two years had passed since Paris stole fair Helen.

A little more time went by and most of the chieftains were happy, because everything seemed to point to a quietening of the situation. Yet there was one among them who could find no peace, and this was Menelaus. Again he began to go from city to city, making speeches to raise up their leaders. He had no trouble persuading his brother, nor were Nestor and Achilles harder to convince. The great heroes were no problem, but there were many others who complained.

"We gave one oath and one oath we responded to," some claimed.

"The gods don't want us to go to Troy," others protested.

"You swore an oath to stand loyal at my side," Menelaus retorted, "so you can leave the gods out of it. No god wants our women snatched from us and our treasuries looted, let alone to see us mocked on top of it. If we do not fight in Troy, if we do not take Helen back and all the valuables they have stolen from us and as much gold besides as men will remember to the end of time, then we will not have done our duty!"

Was it their sense of honour that he touched? Was it the thought of gold? Whatever the reason, little by little they were all persuaded once again. But eight more years were to pass before the fleet was once more massed at Aulis.

Even then a difficulty remained: someone was needed who could lead the ships to Troy with certainty.

Odysseus' opinion was that only Telephus, who was married to one of Priam's daughters, could show them the right way. But Telephus had been left lying wounded in Mysia. How could they find him now? And if they did, how could he be persuaded to guide them to Ilium when Priam was his father-in-law?

In the meantime, however, Telephus boarded a ship of his own accord and set off to find the leaders of the Achaeans, for the wound in his leg was still giving him agony and when he asked the oracle what was to be done, he had received the answer: "Only he who wounded you can cure you."

So now Telephus had come to Greece in search of Achilles. How could he find him, though, and if he did, would he agree to heal the enemy who had wrought such havoc among the Achaean forces and wounded his friend Patroclus? For this reason, when he came ashore he first dressed himself as a poor wanderer and then set off for Mycenae and the palace of Agamemnon.

As was the custom in those days, every passing stranger, whether aristocrat or beggar, would be offered the hospitality of the dinner-table first and only afterwards asked who he was and what he wanted. This is what happened with Telephus. When he had eaten and drunk, Agamemnon himself asked him who he was and what he desired of him.

In reply, the stranger suddenly sprang up and snatched young Orestes from the arms of Clytemnestra, crying:

"I am Telephus – and I will throw this boy into the fire if you do not promise to bring Achilles here to heal my wound. For years now I have suffered unbearable tortures from it, and the oracle told me that only he who wounded me can make me well."

Many leaders were gathered at Mycenae and among them was Achilles.

Agamemnon gave orders for him to be brought.

"I lay down one condition, though," he told Telephus. "We shall heal your wound only if you agree to show us the way to Troy."

He agreed to this, but Achilles refused to make him well again. He could not forget that he had wounded his friend Patroclus.

"I don't know anything about healing wounds," he muttered.

"But you learned medicine from Cheiron," Agamemnon protested. "You made Patroclus' arm as good as new. And now you say you don't know how to deal with this?"

"Anyway, I'm not helping him. If anyone else wants to tend his wounds, then let him do so."

"But the oracle said that only what wounded me could make me well," Telephus insisted.

"Achilles' spear wounded you," Odysseus exclaimed. "Bring it here, Achilles!" And taking the weapon he scraped some flakes of rust off its sharp blade onto Telephus' wounded leg, which healed almost immediately. And so Telephus agreed to lead the Greeks to Troy, although he refused to fight against Priam because he was his wife's father.

THE SACRIFICE OF IPHIGENEIA

Finally everything was ready for the expedition. The army had assembled once again at Aulis. Only one thing delayed the departure of the fleet: there was not a breath of wind. They waited for a breeze to get up, but in vain

"How long will this go on?" many of them began to ask.

"It's clear the gods are against us," others muttered. "We should return to our homes."

The leaders were as worried as their men. Eventually they decided to consult Calchas, the army's mighty seer. And here is what he told them:

"The goddess Artemis is angry with the leader of our forces. She has harboured resentment against him for many years because although Agamemnon always seeks her help whenever he's in need, when the time comes to make offerings he conveniently forgets her. Recently, he added insult to injury. He shot a deer, and as his arrow found its mark from a great distance, he began to boast not even Artemis had skills that could match his. Worst of all, here in the woods at Aulis he shot a wild goat, a sacred animal which Artemis particularly loved. Now her anger has overflowed, and she demands that he recall an old obligation which he still has not fulfilled. He once promised that he would offer her the loveliest being born that year within his kingdom – and as chance would have it, the most beautiful of all turned out to be his baby daughter Iphigeneia. He, of course, forgot his promises to Artemis, to her rage and mortification. But now the time has come for Agamemnon to pay in full. The goddess will not be placated until he sacrifices his daughter Iphigeneia to her. Only then will the wind fill our sails and blow the ships to Troy."

Agamemnon listened horror-struck. There was no point in quarrelling over Calchas' explanation; yet to meekly accept the slaughter of his beloved daughter, that was too terrible to contemplate. No, he would never allow such a thing to happen! Hiding his true thoughts, however, he said:

"Clytemnestra would never accept such a sacrifice."

"Nobody wants this thing to happen," Menelaus replied, "but unless we give the goddess what she demands, how shall we ever leave for Troy?"

"I don't care if we never leave, if it means sacrificing Iphigeneia!" muttered Agamemnon under his breath. Aloud, however, he merely said, "I don't know. One thing is sure, though: her mother will never allow it."

"When it's a goddess laying down the terms, we're not likely to seek the mother's opinion. What's needed is for you to make your mind up."

"Much as I hate the thought I must obey. I am commander of the army and cannot do otherwise. If Clytemnestra agrees to it, I will raise no objections."

"Say it straight out," one of his generals accused him. "You do not intend to obey the goddess."

"Then let's elect another commander," a second suggested.

"Let's make Palamedes our leader!" shouted a third.

Odysseus sprang to his feet.

"If you want Palamedes as commander, then goodbye. I shall pack up and leave." And he made as if to return to his followers.

"Stop, Odysseus. I don't agree that we should change commanders either," said Menelaus, "but Agamemnon must make up his mind here and now."

The commander-in-chief still said nothing.

"Listen, Agamemnon," Odysseus said. "I had no desire at all to help Menelaus, but from the moment that I gave my word, there was no going back on it. Don't think I do not understand you. I know how hard it is for you to tell Iphigeneia she must come here to be sacrificed to Artemis. Even if you're acting on the goddess' orders, you can't put it to her in so many words. There is another way, however. Sit down and write to your wife Clytemnestra, telling her to send Iphigeneia here so you can give her in marriage to Achilles. Pretend you're doing it because the army wants to give him a reward for saving us from the wrath of Telephus, back in Mysia. Only make sure you write that Iphigeneia must come alone, without any female companions — without her mother, that is. Tell her it's not right for the king's wife to be seen in an army camp. And add that she's to send the girl at once, because we're just waiting on this wedding to set off."

Again, Agamemnon did not reply.

Finally it was Menelaus who wrote the letter for him, on a clay tablet.

"Sign it," he told him. "The army is growing restless. Iphigeneia must come here."

"What if Achilles does not agree to have his name mixed up in this? Shouldn't we consult him first?" asked Agamemnon, playing for time.

"And what if he says no?" Odysseus retorted. "How shall we find another way of getting Iphigeneia sent here? Listen, Agamemnon, there is no alternative. You must

..."Say it straight out. You do not intend to obey
the goddess."...

sign."

"Yes, you must sign," the others echoed.

And only then, with a shaking hand, did Agamemnon scratch his name at the foot of the clay tablet.

The letter was sent off, while the high king withdrew into his tent and, falling face down on his couch, burst into bitter tears.

But soon he sprang to his feet once more.

"What have I done?" he cried. "No, I shall not let it happen!" And with these words he took another tablet and scribbled this brief message to Clytemnestra:

'Do not send Iphigeneia. The wedding is off!'

Then he called a trusted servant and told him:

"Take my chariot and horses and make all speed for Mycenae. Deliver this letter into my wife's hands. But take care: nobody must know that I have sent you."

Now Menelaus had feared his brother might have second thoughts, so he kept a careful watch. As soon as he saw Agamemnon's charioteer readying the horses, he set off ahead and lay in wait at a bend in the road. When the chariot came, he stepped out in front of it.

"Stop!" he cried.

The driver had no choice but to obey.

"Give me the letter!" Menelaus commanded.

"I have no letter," said the servant, in a frightened voice.

"Then what is this?" he asked, and pulled from under the servant's cloak the tablet he had been trying to conceal in his armpit. "Now get out of here. But do not go straight back. Put it off as long as you like, and when you do return, tell Agamemnon any story that you please. Tell him I took the letter if you like. It doesn't bother me."

In the end, having let two days go by, Menelaus went alone to Agamemnon.

"Doing this hurt me as much as it will hurt you," he told him, "but there was no other way. Here, take back this letter, and let's think how we can break the news of the sacrifice to Iphigeneia."

"How dare you spy on me and intercept my mail!" screamed Agamemnon, outraged.

This was more than Menelaus could take.

"How dared you send a second letter, when you'd already signed the first?" he retorted. "So you want the expedition called off, eh? We decided on war, Agamemnon, and wars cannot be waged without sacrifices. Not one life, but thousands will be lost in the upholding of our honour, the honour of all the Achaeans. And now the lot has fallen on your daughter, you, the commander-in-chief, step back from the brink! Very well, then; I no longer consider you my brother. I no longer recognise you as high king. Disband the army, since that's what you want, but you'll become the laughing-stock of all your generals – and don't think they will take this humiliation from you. Why, which of them will agree to abandon an expedition which promises glory, treasure and a chance to mete out a bitter lesson to all wife-thieves, whoever they may be!"

Agamemnon's resistance was at an end. He fell weeping into the arms of his brother. "It is hideous," he sobbed. "Iphigeneia is the dearest thing on earth to me!"

Indeed, it was not long before his luckless daughter arrived from Mycenae accompanied by her mother and two girl friends. Agamemnon was caught unprepared. "We'd told her to come alone," he muttered. "This makes things much more difficult."

Iphigeneia ran into her father's embrace.

"Oh, my unfortunate girl!" he cried out, unable to check his words; and two tears rolled down his cheeks.

"But I've come to be married, father. I'm as happy as can be!"

"What words of greeting are these?" her mother added. "Has something happened? You are trembling like a leaf."

"No, no, they were words of joy. I am so deeply moved that the thought of her happiness fills me with dread."

"You're getting your words all mixed up, father!" Iphigeneia cried.

"How can one be stirred by fear at his daughter's happiness? You're out of your mind."

"Out of my mind with joy. Such a wedding! Oh, goddess of the moonlight night, have pity on me!"

"Mother, father is talking nonsense. Something is wrong!"

"One moment you say you're happy, husband, and the next you look miserable. Anyone would think our daughter was going to marry Hades!"

"No, it's Achilles that she's getting, and I'm glad of that. But Hades, too, is a great king – of the underworld."

"Mother, father is making me afraid."

"Fear not, my child, it's only out of happiness. But just

..."Mother, father is talking nonsense. Something
is wrong!"...

tell me this, Agamemnon – what has this wedding got to do with the underworld?"

"I don't know. Don't ask. Anyway, why are you here, when I told you not to come?"

"The greatest day in our daughter's life, and you thought you could keep me away?"

"Don't look on it like that. Ah, well, never mind. Since you insisted on bringing her here in person I will not be angry with you. But this is an army camp. You can't stay any longer. Besides, I shall be here. Everything will be done as it must, and as the gods would wish."

"Oh, father, don't send mother away. I want her by my side."

"I shall stay, my girl. I shall be near you in your joy, and if the gods so wish it, in your sorrow, too."

"If you must, then, stay," said Agamemnon. "After all, this is a wedding and a time of great rejoicing." Then, covering his face with his hands, he withdrew inside his tent lest anyone should see their mighty leader weeping. But Iphigeneia and her mother saw his tears and fell into each other's arms with sobs.

They were still standing there with heavy hearts when they heard footsteps approaching. Turning, they saw a young warrior, handsome as a god, decked in shining armour.

"Forgive me," he murmured, "I did not see you here," and made as if to leave.

"One moment," Clytemnestra said, "perhaps you are..."

"No, I am Achilles, son of Peleus and Thetis," the young

man replied, a little embarrassed.

"And I am Clytemnestra, wife of Agamemnon — and here is Iphigeneia. Yes... Iphigeneia!"

"Delighted to have made your acquaintance; but I am on duty and I'm afraid I cannot stay."

"Wait a moment. I want to meet the man who's going to marry my daughter. Is there anything bad in that?"

"I am delighted to hear that our commander is giving away his daughter. And I agree there's nothing wrong in getting to know one's son-in-law before the wedding; but I'm afraid I really can't help you. I haven't heard anything about it. I don't know who the lucky man will be."

Achilles' words were all it took for Iphigeneia to sink her head upon her mother's shoulders and soak it with tears. If anything, Clytemnestra was more shattered still.

"So they lied when they said they wanted Iphigeneia to come here to be married — and to you at that! She wasn't brought here for her own good. Why did they bring her, then? What evil are they hiding from us?"

Achilles stood thunderstruck by what he heard.

"I am sorry, but I do not understand this at all," he said.

Iphigeneia could bear no more. Leaving her mother, she ran to find her friends, where she could sob her heart out unrestrained.

Clytemnestra gave Achilles a sympathetic look. He was the innocent victim of a plot — a plot in which her daughter was an even greater victim. Exactly what coils was she caught in, though? How could she learn? Just then, who should she see but a faithful servant of hers, now serving with Agamemnon's forces. She called him over.

"I want you to tell me everything you know," she ordered.

"Madam, I am just a servant. Yours, of course, but Agamemnon is my master. It is not fit for me to speak unless he gives the word."

"So you do know, then?"

"I know a lot. I know it all, in fact; but I am afraid to tell."

"If by telling you will do harm, then say nothing. If not, speak out boldly."

"You are right. I can do no greater harm than that which is about to happen. Besides, sooner or later you, Achilles and the unfortunate girl will learn it all. But maybe someone can hear us. Could Iphigeneia be listening?"

"Speak freely. Do not be afraid."

The servant began his tale. He told them all there was to know: for it was he who had set off for Mycenae with the second message, which Menelaus had taken from him.

"Oh, woe is me!" cried Clytemnestra when the servant finished. "Now I know why his wits seemed scrambled when he spoke to us. A hideous crime — and all planned in advance. So I am to lose my precious daughter!"

"No!" cried Achilles. "I will not allow it! They have plotted against me behind my back, and used my name to ensnare an innocent girl. They will have me to reckon with first. Let the fleet rot in Aulis! Let Paris go unpunished! I shall not let this sacrifice take place!"

Suddenly they heard the voice of Iphigeneia behind

them.

"Mother, I feared some great evil and came to find you. I could not help overhearing what was said. But do not be afraid. My father is against this sacrifice and he will find a way to save me."

"Oh, my girl, what terrible misfortune has befallen us. Come, we must try to stir your father's heart. He loves you dearly."

"Yes, mother. He grieves for me as much as you do. His sorrow is even greater than my own. If it is possible, he will save me."

"What do you mean, 'if'? He is the high king!"

"Perhaps that will be the very reason which prevents him, mother."

"If he prefers the trappings of power to his child!"

"I cannot believe that is true."

"I know your father better than you do."

"I ought to be leaving," murmured the servant. "I think I hear my master coming. He must not see me with you."

"I shouldn't stay here either," said Achilles, and he, too, beat a swift retreat.

"Father!" wailed Iphigeneia, as Agamemnon approached. "Why, father? What harm have I done to the Achaean army?"

"What's that you're saying? I do not understand. Or are you foretelling some evil stroke of fortune?"

"She's not foretelling it, she's heard every detail. We have learned the horrible deed you have decided on."

"What are you talking about?"

"Father, you will save me, won't you? I came here to be wedded. Surely you will not let me die instead?"

"So you know it all! It seems someone took pity on me, since my own lips could not pronounce the hideous truth!"

"What now, father?"

"My child, do you think this does not break my heart?"

"It's your decision that concerns us, not your heart! Are you going to sacrifice an innocent creature and her mother's happiness for the sake of Menelaus and his faithless wife? Tell me, have you thought about that? How shall I find the courage to go back to Mycenae with my expectations of a splendid wedding dashed? How shall I face her empty room while you are far away? And tell me this: what shall I say to her younger sisters and little Orestes when they ask me? Shall I tell them she is married? What excuses shall I give if they find my pillow soaked with tears? 'Yes, she is married', I shall tell them, 'but she took Charon for a husband.' And when they ask me how this terrible thing happened, again, what shall I say? Even if I do not tell them it was you who killed her, do you think the secret can be kept for ever? Some day it will come out! Then, when you return, victorious though it may be, how do you think your children will receive you? Even if they overcome their fear, how will you be able to take them in your arms? Have you thought at all of all these things? No, all you fear is that they may choose some other for their leader and that you will lose the glory of your rank!"

"Be silent, woman! It is enough that I have a breaking heart."

"I know how much you love her," she replied. "I would not speak to you at all if I did not. I love all my children dearly but in equal measure. You, too, love them all. Yet you were always especially fond of Iphigeneia. Remember once you held her on your knees and said: 'You are little still, yet I cannot wait to see you happy with a good man worthy of your parents' name?' And she replied, winding her fingers in your beard, 'Do not hurry, father. I am so happy that we are all together. But when that young man takes me from you and the years have passed, I want to take you into my home in your old age, to repay your love and care for me as well as I know how.' That's how she spoke to you, and your eyes filled with tears. Then do you remember how you always told me, 'If I live my life out to its span, I shall ask Iphigeneia to take me in, and when my time has come, it is her I want to close my eyes in death?' Now look what turn fate has taken. That you, of all people... and to Iphigeneia! I did not mean the things I said to you at first, but even so, how could you have agreed? How could you bring yourself to send us such a letter... how? There we were, filled with unsuspecting happiness, convinced the goddess of love herself had chosen such a divine youth as Achilles for us. Our innocent daughter jumped for joy when she read the letter; and when she came, her heart leapt in her breast when she beheld him, as handsome as a god. Now she is doomed to die in the first flush of youth, without ever knowing the delights which the goddess of love so richly showers on rich and poor, immortals and common men alike. Yet you accepted such a fate and decided on the hideous sacrifice. I boil with anger every time I think of it. Enough of that, however. I tell you this, though: only you can save her!"

"I cannot. It is a goddess who commands. At first I would not submit to her wishes. I resisted with all my might, but the army rose against me. All my generals claimed I wanted the expedition to be called off, the kidnappers and thieves left unpunished, and the harsh vengeance of the gods to fall upon us. 'We swore an oath!' they cried. I promised to submit to their demands. The first to pay his blood-toll in this war would be me. I had no choice but to accept. But listen, I hear shouts again! There are many who still believe I will go back on my word. I shall go to see what is afoot. You go back to my tent and console yourselves with tears. I, alas, do not even have the right to weep."

And with these words he hastened towards the spot the shouts were coming from.

"It is over, mother," Iphigeneia sighed. "Father can do nothing now. My fate is sealed. But be of good heart – I shall endure until the end."

"All is not lost. There is hope still. Let us go to seek Achilles."

"No, mother, there is no one we can turn to. Don't you hear the shouts?"

"What do they mean?"

"They mean that all are crying for my blood and Achilles cannot save me. But, look. Here he comes."

"Tell us, Achilles, what are the soldiers shouting?"

Clytemnestra asked in fear.

"For the sacrifice to be carried out immediately!"

"What do their leaders say?"

"Exactly the same words, alas!"

"Then let it be. Yes, immediately!" Iphigeneia broke in. "Life is sweet and death a black shadow, but this agony must end for all of us."

Yet she gazed at Achilles with such bitter disappointment in her eyes that he cried out:

"No, over my dead body!"

"I will not let it come to that," said Iphigeneia.

"What are you saying, girl?" her mother interrupted. "They will never dare cross swords with Achilles."

"They have dared already," the young hero answered.

"But you have the Myrmidons behind you. Who will dare resist you?"

"They will be the first to hurl stones at me."

"So you are alone?"

"There is no one on my side."

"Then all is lost, my girl."

Yet Achilles still clung to one hope.

"All is not lost," he said. "I am the son of Thetis and Peleus. I shall stand before her with my sword in hand. Let them dare!"

"Listen to me," Iphigeneia broke in, "and you, too, mother, listen. The time has come for me to say what has long been turning in my mind. This sacrifice must be made. A goddess insists upon it, and the whole army. The fleet must sail for Troy. Achilles, you are no longer guided by your mind. Your heart has gone out to me just as mine has clung to yours. Perhaps that is why you cannot see that what matters above all is that the ravagers be punished. If the abduction of Helen slighted Menelaus alone, it would be a matter of little consequence. As things are, Paris has humiliated all of Greece, and he must not go unpunished. We cannot bow our heads to this barbarity. Those who meekly swallow insults are to be despised. That is why I shall go of my own accord to the altar of Artemis. I shall bare my throat unaided to the priest's keen knife, and with my blood I shall placate the goddess. Then Artemis will raise the wind the ships require, and the gods will aid the Achaeans to besiege high-towered Troy and return victorious to their homeland."

Achilles listened in awed respect. Torn between astonishment and admiration, he could find no words to dissuade her. Iphigeneia, the girl who had so suddenly won his heart, was destined to lay down her life.

"You are right," he told her. "It was as you said – I was blinded by love. Yet now I have a deeper understanding of that which has been taken from me, and the sacrifice which but a short while ago I could not bear the thought of, I now accept with pride. In this brief space I have loved and lost a valiant spirit."

Iphigeneia stayed no longer. She bade her mother and Achilles farewell.

"I am going to find my father. I have delayed too long already," she said.

Her unhappy mother, seeing that further words would be

of no avail, withdrew to her tent. She would not emerge from it till all was over.

Dusk was falling when her faithful servant ran to seek her out.

"My lady," he cried, "A miracle beyond belief has happened!"

Clytemnestra came running from the tent. A wind was blowing.

"If it had been the miracle I hoped for," she told herself, "Iphigeneia would have been the first to bring the news to me."

"Your daughter has been taken by the goddess!" the servant gasped. "Hear how it happened. She bared her throat to the knife so willingly that all who saw it wondered at her courage. As the priest raised his arm to strike the blow, we all lowered our eyes, to avoid witnessing the dreadful sight. We held our breath and waited. You could have heard a leaf fall. Then, suddenly, we heard the sound of the knife, quite clearly, and at that very instant a loud voice crying, 'A miracle! A miracle!' We raised our eyes at once, but the girl was nowhere to be seen. In her place, at the priest's feet, a deer twitched in its death-throes. We stood there numb with shock, then Calchas climbed up to the altar. Stretching his hand before him, he announced: 'Mighty Agamemnon and leaders of the Achaeans, hear my words! The goddess did not wish her altar to be stained with this innocent maiden's blood. She has taken Iphigeneia with her, far away to the distant land of Taurus, where she will be her priestess. The goddess' anger is placated. You see the evidence around you: the leaves are rustling on the trees and a wind has blown up off the land. The fleet, with all our troops on board, can now set sail for Troy. Let us go forth with courage and faith in final victory.'"

The servant's tale was ended but Clytemnestra could not believe his words.

"A beautiful story, fellow, but only to console me, I fear," she told him. "This 'miracle' you speak of is too hard to believe."

"But everybody saw it. Look, here comes Agamemnon. He will tell you for himself."

"Our pain is softened, wife. Our daughter is in the goddess' hands and will know eternal life. Now we shall set sail with the army. Troy will be taken, its towers will fall, and on our return we shall all celebrate the great victory."

NINE YEARS OF WAR

Beneath a towering plane tree, which overhung a fountain, the Achaeans were sacrificing their choicest oxen to the gods before setting out for Troy. Suddenly a great red-spotted snake darted from the roots of the tree and slithered up to its highest branch, where there was a sparrow's nest containing eight chicks with their mother hovering around them. The snake swallowed all eight of them and then devoured the mother sparrow, too. The moment it did so, it was turned to stone. The seer Calchas then said that the nine birds which the snake had eaten were a sign from Zeus that this war would go on for nine years and that Troy would only be taken in the tenth. They all rejoiced to hear the great soothsayer tell them clearly that they would be victorious in Troy, but no one wanted to believe that the war would last so long.

The sacrifice completed, the whole army boarded ship and after the traditional libations to the gods, the fleet set sail. It did not head straight for Troy, however, but for Delos, where they would take on supplies.

This island was ruled by Anius, son of Apollo. Anius had a son, Andrus, who became king of the island which still bears his name, and three daughters, Spermo, Elais and Oeno. Seeking protection from Dionysus for them, Anius appointed the three maidens as his priestesses, and in return for the services they rendered him, the god gave each of them a wondrous gift. Thus, whatever Spermo touched was turned to corn, whatever Elais laid her fingers on was transformed into oil, and Oeno had the power to change things into wine.

It is not surprising, then, that Agamemnon led his fleet to Delos. Anius extended a warm welcome there to him and all the leaders of the Achaeans, while his daughters willingly gave them all the army needed, and in unlimited amounts. Besides this, their father Anius, who was a renowned soothsayer, prophesied as Calchas had done that Troy would be taken in the tenth year. He even told them to spend nine years on Delos and only then to voyage on to Troy, thus conquering it without a long campaign. Yet how could these seasoned generals believe that Ilium could be taken while they idled their time away on Delos? So they rejected the soothsayer's advice and decided to put out to sea once more.

Today, of course, we know that oracles and the like have

no foundation in logic. Yet here is one of those cases where even in those distant days an oracle's truth was doubted by its hearers, and the case of Anius is not the only one in ancient literature. However, if today we do not believe that everything is ordained by the gods, this does not mean that we do not enjoy the air of mystery which the fertile imagination on these long-dead writers has bequeathed to us.

While the Achaeans had taken on a good store of food and drink at Delos, Agamemnon was not yet satisfied. "If this war turns out to be a long one," he declared, "we will find ourselves in need of fresh supplies." For this reason he ordered Menelaus and Odysseus to go secretly at night and bring Anius' three daughters to the ships.

Obedient to Agamemnon, they went and brought the maidens back in chains. On setting sail, they freed them from their shackles, whereupon they escaped by diving into the sea and swimming all the way to Andros where their brother was king. Agamemnon responded by threatening him with war if he did not hand his sisters over. He refused, but the three girls decided to give themselves up rather than let blood be shed. Once they were back on board, however, they begged the god Dionysus to help them, and this he did by transforming them into doves, which fluttered up into the heavens and flew back to their father. From that day since, no one has ever harmed the doves of Delos.

The fleet made its second call at Nea, the island of the nymph Chryse, a small islet off the coast of Lemnos which does not exist today.

Chryse, who was queen of this island, ruled all the seas

round Troy and the Hellespont with her fleet, and so the Achaean ships stopped over there to make sacrifices at the altar of Athena, the goddess who protected the island. Thus they would win the favour of the queen, and their ships would be allowed to approach Troy unimpeded. However, before the sacrifice took place, a serious accident occurred. As they were clearing the altar of undergrowth, a snake darted out and bit the leg of Philoctetes, the famous archer to whom Heracles had given his arrows before dying. The area round the bite quickly swelled and darkened. The hero groaned with the pain of it, and soon the air was foul with the stench of the pus which started oozing from the punctures. Before long his condition was so serious that the army could no longer bear either his sobs of pain or the vile odour which the wound gave off.

So, with heavy hearts, they were obliged to pick up Philoctetes in his sleep and take him to a deserted beach on Lemnos, where they left him. At his side, they put adequate supplies of food and his bow and arrows, in case, with the help of the gods, he should ever recover from the bite and need them. Thus they sailed for Troy leaving behind them no common soldier, but a hero armed with Heracles' deadly arrows dipped in the blood of the Lernaean Hydra. A day would come when they would need them desperately, and bitterly regret having abandoned him on Lemnos. They would sail back to retrieve him, but only after nine whole years had passed.

Lemnos was not far from the Trojan shores and the distance was soon covered; but as they drew near they saw

they would first have to subdue the island of Tenedos,
which lay off the coast of Troy. The king of this island was
Tenes, a close friend of Priam's. Tenes was a man of
mighty strength, and he attempted to prevent the army
coming ashore by sheer force of muscle. But Achilles
jumped into the shallows at the very moment Tenes was
lifting a great boulder to hurl it at the ships. He threw his
javelin straight into his chest and killed him. Now Thetis
had warned Achilles to be careful lest by any mischance he
kill a son of Apollo, for the god's anger would not be
appeased until he in turn had despatched the murderer to
the underworld. As fate would have it, Tenes was indeed
Apollo's child, but by the time Achilles learned this it was
far too late.

Having killed Tenes, the Achaeans conquered all the
island and then made camp beside the sea. Facing them, not
far from the coast, rose many-towered Troy.

The Greek leaders decided to send a group of represen-
tatives over from Tenedos to speak to Priam and see if their
differences could not be resolved without recourse to war.

Menelaus, Palamedes and Odysseus went to Ilium. The
three leaders were received by Antenor, wise counsellor of
the king of Troy. Having wined and dined them at his
house, he and his twelve sons accompanied them to the
people's assembly, where Priam was waiting with all his
sons and a large body of citizens.

Menelaus spoke first. He recounted how he had welcomed Paris to his home with open arms, and with what
low cunning the latter had repaid his hospitality. He de-

manded only that Helen be returned to him with his stolen treasure, and then the Achaeans would depart in peace.

"What about Hesione, though?" retorted Priam. "By what right do you keep my sister hostage in Salamis all these long years? How do you expect justice from us, when you were the first to act unjustly?"

"We committed no injustice," Palamedes answered. "Telamon and Heracles saved Hesione from certain death. She followed Telamon of her own free will and became his wife. That is the truth of the matter."

Then Odysseus spoke in his turn. With great intelligence and persuasiveness he stressed the benefits of peace and the hideous consequences of war. Summing up, he told them:

"Peace is the light and life itself; it is the bread and salt of our existence; peace is love and creativity. War is ruin and despair; it is fire and the blackness of death. War is good only for the crows and vultures!"

Odysseus' wise words made a deep impression on the assembled people. There were some his speech displeased, however, and none more than Paris.

"I am not handing the fair Helen over when she is the gift of a goddess, not only to me but to the whole of Troy."

And many of his brothers shouted: "We shall not give her back!"

"Listen," said Antenor. "If we do not return Helen, and all the stolen treasure, we shall be supporting an unjust cause. Then Ilium may be reduced to smouldering ruins. Paris may have committed a rash deed, but that is no reason for us all to lose our heads and to plunge into the greatest

...Odysseus stressed the benefits of peace and the hideous
consequences of war...

madness of all — the folly of war."

Paris and many of his brothers gave Antenor an ugly look. One of them, Helenus, stepped forward.

"I say we give them nothing," he declared. "Why suffer such humiliation? We shall be the winners in this war, and it will be a mighty victory. When we have smashed the Achaean army at our gates, their cities will fall beneath our feet, all of them, and mighty Troy will become yet mightier still."

Rash words and vain predictions! But it was not his fault. Helenus may have been a seer, like his sister Cassandra, yet when the goddess Hera put words into his mouth his vision was clouded. Troy was not destined to escape destruction, so in the end all sided with the foolish Helenus and not with wise Antenor. As if that were not enough, another of Priam's sons, Deiphobus, leapt to his feet crying, "Death to the foreigners!" And baring his sword he urged his brothers to fall upon the three Greek spokesmen.

"That will only happen over my dead body," roared Antenor. "Woe betide us if we scorn the sacred rules of hospitality!" He ran to place himself between them and the visitors and all his twelve sons followed.

"In the name of the gods, stop!" cried Priam to his children. Hector took his side.

"Get back, quickly!" he cried. "Heaven help us if we come to this!"

Antenor hastily led the foreigners to their ship. Giving them his hand, this wise and noble Trojan said:

"If I spoke in your defence it was because your cause is

just. Yet I failed to persuade anyone. Now duty calls me to
defend our homeland, even if it costs my life."

The three leaders bade him a warm goodbye. When they
were on board Palamedes said, looking back at Antenor:

"This man respects both justice and his duty. Men such
as he are too valuable to waste in war."

When they returned to Tenedos and recounted what had
taken place in Troy, the Greeks' rage swelled and they
thirsted for revenge. Preparations for the invasion were put
in hand at once.

Meanwhile, however, Odysseus and Achilles had fallen
out. The former insisted that Troy should be taken by craft
and cunning stealth, while the latter was for boldly storm-
ing it. Their argument grew increasingly violent, till at last
they came to blows and the other leaders came running up
to separate them. Yet there was one who did so with a look
of satisfaction on his face. This was Agamemnon, who
remembered that an oracle had foretold Ilium would be
taken if two brave leaders of the Achaeans first came to
blows. Before the heroes' wrath had even cooled, he
ordered the troops to embark immediately, sail quickly to
the opposite shore and, without losing an instant, march on
Troy and take the city by storm. His haste was in vain,
however. How was he to know that the quarrel which the
oracle spoke of was not this but another, far worse one
which would take place between himself and Thetis' son
nine years later and bring great misfortune on the Achaeans?

When the fleet reached the shore, the Trojans were al-

ready waiting for them. At their head was Hector, distinguished by his gleaming armour and the crest of horsehair
on his helmet. Agamemnon's orders were to leap ashore at
once, but a prophesy placed an obstacle in the way. The
goddess. Thetis had told Achilles to beware, for the first
invader to touch the soil of Troy would also be the first to
die. The whole army knew of this, and so each man hesi-
tated. Yet one of them, Protesilaus, the son of Iphiclus,
longed to be first to leap upon the Trojans. He wished to
win the glory of being the first among the Achaeans to give
battle against the enemy, even if it cost him his life. Then
he thought of Laodameia, his lovely bride. He remembered
they had had time for but one night of married bliss. He
recalled the moment of his departure, when she had clung
sobbing to his neck, trying to prevent him from going off to
war. Next he thought of his house in Phylace, which he had
left half-built, and finally of his father, old king Iphiclus,
who was left without another child to care for him, since
both his sons had sailed with their forty ships for Troy.

While all this was turning through his mind, who should
leap from the ship but Odysseus. Throwing his shield upon
the sand, he jumped and landed on it, calling to the Achaeans to come ashore. Taken by surprise, Protesilaus sprang
after him and charged with irresistible force upon the
enemy. He wished to protect this Ithacan hero, who, according to the prophesy, must be the first to die. Protesilaus
fought like a lion. He killed numerous Trojans and was so
wild with battle-lust that he even dared to pit his strength
against Hector's, without pausing to consider how superior

...Taken by surprise, Protesilaus sprang after him...

a warrior he was. The mighty Trojan's heavy war-spear
caught him full in the chest and so he became the first of
the Achaeans to fall dead in battle. The crafty Odysseus
had sidetracked fate by taking care to remain upon his
shield until the moment when Protesilaus, jumping from
the ship, became the first to actually touch the soil of Troy
and thus the first to die as the oracle had foretold. A hero
torn between his love of life and fame had been sacrificed
to make the Achaeans come ashore.

    Indeed, once Protesilaus had set the example, the Ar-
gives poured from their ships like ants. The Trojans put up
a heroic resistance, clinging stubbornly to their positions,
and there were many dead and wounded on each side. Then
Achilles joined the fight. Cycnus faced him fearlessly.
Being a son of Poseidon, he could be wounded by neither
spear nor sword and had already slain many Achaeans. The
Trojans were confident that he would be able to hold
Thetis' son at bay. Charging up on Achilles, Cycnus flung
his sharp-pointed spear. But the latter took its force upon
his sturdy shield and hurled his deadly lance full pitch at
Cycnus. What happened next left him gaping in surprise:
the lance curved in its flight and turned away from its
target. Then Achilles lunged at Cycnus with his sword, but
quickly realised that could not wound him either. Angrily
tossing it aside, he fell on him with his bare hands. A
desperate struggle now ensued between them, but for all
Cycnus' great strength there was not a stronger man than
his adversary in the whole world. Caught in Achilles'
choking grip, Cycnus realised that his end had come.

Before dying, he begged his father not to let Achilles strip him of his armour. Poseidon heard and transformed him into a beautiful, great white bird. From then on, Cycnus, or the swan, has flown across the skies. Yet despite the loss of his son, Poseidon was not angry with the Achaeans. Ever since the time Laomedon had insulted him, he had been filled with such hatred for the Trojans that only the destruction of their city would appease it.

After this victory, Achilles charged on forward. All the other generals did likewise. Behind them followed a huge mass of men, for in the meantime the whole army had disembarked from the ships. The Achaeans were now exerting fearsome pressure, but the Trojans, fighting for the very survival of their homeland, laid down their lives without counting the cost. It was Hector, who, seeing that resistance was impossible in the face of such overwhelming forces, gave the order for general retreat which saved the army from destruction. Holding firm their ranks, the Trojans withdrew in good order to their city. They closed the heavy, studded gates, mounted the walls, and from this commanding position kept the enemy at a distance with their arrows. The first battle had ended. If Troy had not been taken immediately, as Agamemnon had counted upon, it was still a victory, and one that permitted the Argives to install themselves on Trojan soil, which was no mean feat. When the fighting was over, the Achaeans behaved with chivalry towards the Trojans, permitting them to come and take their dead away for burial.

Protesilaus was buried with full military honours. Games

were held in his memory and his body was laid to rest in the Thracian peninsula, beyond the Hellespont. The hero's grave was soon green with elm trees planted by the forest nymphs. They grew taller and sturdier by the day, but each time they reached a height where they could see above the surrounding trees and across the Hellespont to the fortress walls of Troy they would wither and die, then grow up from their roots once more. The unlucky hero, so the poets said, could not bear to look upon the city on whose account he had never returned to his beloved Laodameia and the homeland which he longed for.

But Laodameia did not outlive her husband of one day. Unable to endure the separation, she made a likeness of him out of wax and sat with it by the hour. When her father learned of this, instead of showing pity he took the image and hurled it in the fire. Seeing it melt and sputter into flame, Laodameia knew that Protesilaus would never again return from distant Troy. Maddened with grief, she threw herself into its fiery embrace and was consumed together with the likeness of the man she loved. She killed herself, men say, at the very instant Protesilaus fell dead upon the battlefield of Troy.

Next day the Achaeans dragged their ships ashore and set up camp. In the middle, on a flattened knoll, they pitched a big pavilion for their leader Agamemnon. From this position he could keep the whole army under observation. It was also important to give added protection to the flanks; thus Achilles was assigned quarters on the left and Great Ajax on the right. Odysseus decided to put his tent

near Agamemnon's, for it was there the war-councils and
assemblies of the troops were to be held, and Odysseus,
who loved to make his voice heard in discussions, was
determined to miss not one of these.

When all was ready, Agamemnon called his generals
into conference.

"I have asked you here," he said, "because I propose we
make an immediate attack and take Troy by storm. The
enemy is tired and weak. We must act fast, before he
regroups his forces and calls in reinforcements."

They all agreed with Agamemnon, who continued to
believe that they could conquer Troy simply because two
Danaid chiefs had quarrelled. This prophesy he remembered clearly; the other, which said that Troy would not be
taken until ten years had passed, had completely slipped his
mind.

The attack took place, but it was not successful. A second and a third one followed, again with no result. The
towering ramparts which the gods had built were unassail-
able. The Trojan archers were fighting from the battle-
ments, picking off the Achaean warriors one by one; and
although the latter retaliated with their bows, the enemy
were well-protected by their arrow-slits. When it at last
became clear that Troy could not be taken by a frontal
assault, the Greeks began to besiege the city, in the belief
they could wear down their foes by hunger and other
deprivations. Yet the siege proved ineffective too, for Troy
backed onto a hilly, wooded area, which made it possible
for the defenders to bring in supplies, while on the other

hand the Achaeans' stores of food were steadily diminish-
ing. Their army was a large one, far too large to be maintained by whatever victuals they could lay their hands on
close to Ilium. There was only one solution: to make raids
on neighbouring or even distant cities, as indeed they did.
However, this weakened the army, when a part of it was
constantly obliged to be out foraging far away from Troy.
Thus the war stretched into a long drawn out affair, and
increasing numbers of the Achaeans began to remember the
prophesy they had once taken so lightly – that Priam's city
would not be taken until the tenth year of campaigning.

In the meantime, the existence of yet another prophesy
was learned of, one known only to the Trojans up till now.
This foretold that Troy would never be taken at all, if
Troilus could attain the age of twenty. Troilus, the youngest
son of Priam, was then a lad of fifteen and it was said that
when he reached his twentieth year he would become
Hector's equal at leading men in war, or even better still,
and then Troy would have nothing more to fear. Indeed, he
was already a skilled horseman and practised with his
weapons every day. The Trojans should have taken care to
see he was not killed before his time, but instead they
treated him with indulgent admiration every time he
climbed up on the ramparts with his bow and took aim at
some enemy, or, worse still, rode out unconcerned beyond
the walls to the spring of Thymbraean Apollo to water his
horse.

All the while, the Greeks were planning how to kill him.
They learned that he was in the habit of leaving the safety

of the city and riding to Apollo's spring, but the spot was sacred. Other Trojans went there to draw water, too, and the Achaeans never harassed them, for to desecrate this holy place would bring the god's wrath down upon their heads. Nevertheless, Achilles was determined to do away with him.

"I shall ambush him upon the pathway leading to the spring," he said. "That is not hallowed ground. Besides, if we let Troilus live we shall go on pouring out our blood in Troy for nothing."

From the moment Achilles took this decision, Priam's son was doomed. On the fateful day, Troilus set out on horseback for the spring escorting his sister Polyxena, who was going there to fill a pitcher with water. Suddenly Achilles stepped out into his path. The moment he set eyes on him, Troilus dug his heels into his horse's flanks and made off at a gallop, while Polyxena let the water-jar fall from her hand and stood there as if frozen.

"What beauty!" Achilles murmured to himself, and stopped dead in his tracks. Indeed, he almost forgot the purpose he had come for. But he soon came out of his trance and set off after her brother. Now the hunt was on.

Priam's young son was famous for his skill on horseback, but Achilles had an equal reputation as a runner. On the face of it, it seemed impossible that the son of Peleus could catch up with Troilus. After all, no runner can make headway against a strong horse running at full gallop. Yet Achilles proved so fleet-footed that the young horseman could not draw away from him. Nor could he get back to

Troy, for as often as he tried the son of Thetis blocked his way. Troilus' only hope was that Achilles' pace would flag, but instead it was his horse that first began to tire. There was no hope now for the Trojan lad, but he did not despair. They were drawing steadily closer to the sacred spring, with its altar to Thymbraean Apollo. If he could only reach the spot, Achilles would not dare to kill him. Now the altar was in sight; one last desperate spurt and Troilus would be saved. But at the very moment he was tensing himself to leap upon it from the horse, Achilles' spear struck home. Troilus fell dead beside the altar and his red blood stained the holy place of sacrifice.

Back in Troy, they saw the horse returning with no rider and knew what had befallen him. Three of Priam's sons brought his lifeless corpse back into the city, and all Ilium wept as if it had been Hector himself that they had lost.

For all this, the Trojans did not give up hope. Numerous gods supported them, and the defiling of Thymbraean Apollo's shrine would not go unpunished. Achilles had indeed incurred Apollo's wrath, and not for the first time, with the result that little by little, from being an enemy of the Trojans the god became their greatest friend. For in this war it was not only men that fought but gods as well – indeed, with greater stubbornness than mortals. The truth is that this cursed conflict would not have broken out at all had the gods not willed it first, and a just peace would long since have been agreed upon had they not prevented it. It was the gods, then, and the ruthless Fates who laid down what men's destinies would be, and who controlled their every deed, sometimes to good ends and sometimes evil. That, at least, was what people believed in those days.

Troilus was not the only one of Priam's sons to be ambushed by Achilles. The other was Lycaon, who was cutting rods from a wild fig-tree to use them in his chariot wheels when he was suddenly confronted by the feared Achaean. Unprepared to face him, Lycaon went down on his knees and begged for mercy.

"My father will give you all the gold you want if you spare my life," he promised.

"You can keep your life – but not where you'll ever run into me again," replied Achilles. "As for your father's gold, let him hang onto it until the day he loses everything!"

And taking Lycaon prisoner, he showed him what his first remark had meant by handing him over to Patroclus to sell to Euneus, king of Lemnos, as a slave. This monarch, by the way, was the son of Jason and Hypsipyle. However, it was not long before Lycaon managed to make his way back to Troy. When Achilles heard the news he was furious with himself for not having slain him there and then – "but he'll not escape if he crosses my path again," he swore.

As time went on, the need to ensure food and supplies for the army grew ever more pressing. Raids on various towns to secure booty now became the most important military operations. Some of these swelled to the proportions of campaigns. Nearly all the cities on the Asian coast of the Aegean and the towns of Thrace and many islands fell prey to the invaders. Achilles alone took and looted twenty-three of them. Of course, these raids were really acts of piracy, but in those days were not seen as such but as regular acts of war requiring heroism and self-sacrifice, which brought lasting glory to those who returned victorious to camp with livestock, corn, rich booty and young women to be slaves.

In one such operation, Achilles met with fierce resistance. For weeks he had been besieging the city of Monenia, but its high walls held out against him strongly. He had already decided he would lift the siege when a girl threw an apple to him from the ramparts. Achilles picked it up and found the following words scratched on its surface: "Do not leave. The city will surrender for lack of water." So the siege was kept up and two days later Monenia opened its gates to the invaders. When Achilles entered the town, the girl – named Pedase – ran to his side and he asked her why she had given away its secret.

"Out of admiration for you," came the reply. "I saw you from the castle and fell in love. Once that had happened, how could I not help you?" She said this hoping that Achilles would appreciate her deed and make her his wife.

Now the great hero would never have wanted a woman at his side who, however much her act had helped him, was tainted with betrayal of her homeland. All the same he did not wish her name to be forgotten, so he renamed the city Pedasus after the girl with whose help he had conquered it.

In another siege, a similar story had a different and tragic end.

The son of Peleus was struggling with his Myrmidons to besiege the town of Mithymna on Lesbos. This, too, was a

...Achilles alone took and looted twenty-three towns...

tough nut to crack. But when the king's daughter, Peisidice, caught sight of Achilles from the ramparts, she sent her old nurse with a promise of help on condition that he marry her. Achilles seized the opportunity and said he would accept. Then Peisidice secretly opened one of the gates and the Myrmidons came surging into the city. In a savage mood after the long, frustrating siege, they immediately began to slay and loot, while Peisidice, coolly indifferent to what was going on before her eyes, led Achilles and the Myrmidons up to the palace. With the same scornful calm she watched them kill her royal father and all the members of her family. Then, when the slaughter was accomplished, she ran to Achilles panting for the reward she lusted after. The payment she received was not the one expected: in disgust, the son of Peleus ordered his men to stone the slut to death, the most degrading form of execution that was known.

But the foray which had the most important consequences for our story took place in the south-east of the Trojan territory. There Achilles first attacked the city of Thebe, ruled by Eëtion, father of Hector's wife Andromache. Eëtion and his seven sons put up a heroic resistance and it required a bloody struggle, in which the king and all his sons were killed, to take the city. Nevertheless, Achilles respected the corpse of Andromache's father, burying it with all its armour and raising a high mound above the grave.

In this city, Achilles captured valuable booty and many lovely slaves. Among them was the beautiful Chryseis, daughter of Chryses, priest of Apollo, who was in Thebe merely by chance, having gone there to offer sacrifices at the altar of Artemis.

From Thebe, Achilles made for tall mount Ida, on whose slopes Priam's son Mestor was overseer of the numerous shepherds who grazed his father's flocks. On the other side of the same mountain were the grazing grounds of Priam's cousin Anchises, who was king of Dardanus. His herdsmen took their orders from Aeneas, his son by Aphrodite. Achilles first fell on Priam's flocks, killing Mestor and taking all the animals. Then he made off over the mountain for Anchises' herds, which fell into his hands together with the herdsmen. Only Aeneas managed to escape and he sought refuge in the neighbouring city of Lyrnessus, which was ruled by a friend and ally of his father by the name of Mynes. They put up a heroic fight to save the city, but Achilles and his Myrmidons swept through it like a raging fire and Mynes, his brother and his three sons were killed. Aeneas would have met his death there, too, had Aphrodite not spirited him away in time. Here, as in Thebe, the victors carried off rich spoils, chief among which, again, was a large number of lovely maidens. Among them, and lovelier than them all, was queen Briseis, daughter of Briseus, priest of Dionysus.

Achilles returned in triumph from this campaign, his soldiers leading countless beasts, his chariots loaded with rich booty and his waggons over-flowing with supplies of every kind. In the midst of this abundance were the love-liest girls of Thebe and Lyrnessus.

When the spoils of war and the slave-girls were shared out, the army presented Achilles with Briseis as a prize; to their commander-in-chief, Agamemnon, they gave Chryseis, the only one who could be compared to her in worth and beauty.

Meanwhile, Aeneas had gone to his father after the destruction of Lyrnessus and begged to be given command of the Dardanian army to go and fight at Hector's side. Anchises gave his consent.

"Go, my son," he told him. "We are threatened, too — and besides, it is our duty. The Trojans and the Dardanians are one people; and let whatever fate the gods may have in store for Ilium be shared by Dardanus as well."

Other races now came to help the Trojans. Many of them were from distant parts of Asia, where men spoke foreign tongues. They came because they placed great store in a powerful and wealthy Troy and wished to court her friendship. An outstanding place among these allies was held by the Lycians, who were led by Sarpedon, a son of Zeus. From Europe, too, help came for Priam: the Thracians and the Ciconians and, from further away, the Paeonians, a people who lived in the land watered by the river Axios: 'broad-flowing river, the fairest in the world' as Homer calls it.

Now the Trojans had a mighty force at their disposal, perhaps as great as the Achaean host which was permanently encamped under the walls of Troy. And since neither army was more powerful than the other, the years went by without an end to the war being anywhere in sight. Little by little, a sense of hopelessness began to creep into the Danaid ranks.

"When will this war end?" many of them asked.

"We shall never see our homes again!" others replied.

"Our leaders only care about themselves!" some said.

"And they get all the loot worth having. We only get the crumbs!"

"And half the time, not even those!" some others shouted.

So their resentment grew until one day a huge crowd gathered in front of Agamemnon's tent, demanding with angry shouts that they all return to Greece at once.

Agamemnon reassured the men with promises, while Odysseus used his powers of persuasion.

"Now we have started something, we must bring it to a finish," said the hero from Ithaca. "Soon we shall be entering our tenth year of war, and so the signs all say, this will be the year in which we conquer Troy. We have been very patient, but we shall need a little patience yet if we wish to return to our homes with heads erect and holding up the spoils of war — and not slink back empty-handed, with our tails between our legs."

Many of them shook their heads dubiously at his words. What else were they to do, however? It seemed there was no other solution.

Luckily the unpleasant atmosphere was considerably lightened by Palamedes, the son of Nauplius, from Euboea, the one who had seen through Odysseus' feigned madness.

So that no one would be unfairly treated when rations

were served out, this clever and inventive man thought up and constructed the first scales. Then he made sure the men who needed to learned writing and arithmetic, so that everything important could be written down and proper order established. He even ensured that sentries and patrols were sent out according to a duty roster, so there could be no cause for complaint. It was Palamedes who invented lighthouses to protect the Achaean ships and enable them to find their way back home after long missions. He even concerned himself with the soldiers' entertainment, devising various games to help them spend their free time pleasantly. In fact, if you look in the archaeological museum in Athens you will find some dice with Palamedes' head painted on them. This ingenious hero thought up so many other things that he is said to have become the best-loved of all the Achaean leaders.

But lean days came again. Once more food grew perilously short and the portions, fair as they may now have been, were microscopic. Achilles was tied up with some distant siege, so Agamemnon ordered Odysseus to go to Thrace and bring back whatever food he found. Yet when Odysseus returned, he brought nothing with him but despair.

"Not even one sack of grain?" asked Palamedes in astonishment.

"Don't talk to me as if I didn't know my business. Why don't you go, and let's see what you can bring back."

"Very well, I shall!"

He went – and returned within a matter of days, his ships

piled high with food of every kind: grain, wine, oil, cows and sheep. Odysseus' honour was deeply wounded; but the one who most resented Palamedes' success was Agamemnon. He had seen him as a potential rival since the day his name had been put forward as the Achaeans' new commander, and time and again whispers had reached his ears that if Palamedes were their leader the expedition would have a very different fortune. After this latest exploit, he was not only jealous but afraid.

More than once he told those closest to him that he feared the army might make Palamedes their new commander-in-chief.

"Then all of us will be put out to grass!" he warned.

Then, suddenly, the horrid news fell like a thunderbolt.

"Palamedes is a traitor!"

The charge was false, but it did its work and sealed the brilliant hero's fate. What a vile plot it was! And with what satanic cunning they laid the hideous accusation at his feet!

In the dead of night, someone crept into Palamedes' tent while he was absent and buried a huge sum in gold beneath the floor. Then he wrote a letter which read: 'Palamedes, this gold which I have sent you is in payment for the information that you gave me – Priam.' After this, a Phrygian warrior was taken prisoner by a patrol and told: 'We shall spare your life if you give this sealed letter to your leader.' The Phrygian had scarcely set off on his mission when he fell into an ambush set for him. He was killed and the letter found on his body was brought to the Achaean headquarters. It was a devilish plan, and executed perfectly.

The letter was read out to all the leaders.

"This is not possible!" gasped one.

"Incredible!" another added.

"We must go and search his tent," a third voice cried.

They went there, dug – and found the gold. It was beyond belief, but they could not deny the evidence of their own eyes. The hero was dragged before a military tribunal on charges of high treason.

"Speak! Confess your guilt!"

"I am innocent."

"Then how come Priam wrote this letter to you?"

"I do not know."

"How did the gold get in your tent?"

"I do not know."

"You are a traitor!"

"I am innocent."

"Death to the traitor!"

"Death!"

Palamedes was put to death by stoning, the most horrible and degrading way a man could die. This was a punishment reserved for traitors – and they imposed it on a hero. Before he expired, he managed to gasp out these last words:

"Oh, truth, how I grieve for you! You have died before me!"

Even in death the Achaeans sought to dishonour Palamedes: they would not allow him to be buried, but tossed his body to the hounds and birds of prey.

Achilles ran to stop the evil deed.

"Let anyone who dares try to prevent me!" he cried out.

...The hero was dragged before a military tribunal on charges of high treason....

Ajax, the son of Telamon, hastened to support him.

But it was not only these two who refused to believe that Palamedes was a traitor. There were many other warriors who did not hide their scepticism, and in the end muttering could be heard on every hand: "Palamedes was the victim of a foul conspiracy."

Where did the guilt lie, however? Rumours soon began to spread. It was Odysseus, who could never stomach him, many of them said. It was Agamemnon, who was afraid of him, others whispered furtively. And if, as it seems, the latter were right then Agamemnon had won a double victory. There were two outstandingly intelligent leaders in the Achaean forces whom he had every cause to fear – and by murdering the one he had cast the shadow of men's doubts upon the other.

Odysseus may have been a crafty man, but he was no villain. Agamemnon was the evil one, and ruthless, too. If he had become commander of the army he owed it to the fact that he ruled over Mycenae with its fabulous wealth in gold, and held Zeus' famous sceptre. Unfortunately, it was on the sceptre's account that everyone was now obliged to obey him and find excuses for his lawlessness.

The story does not end here, though – punishment was coming.

When Nauplius learned of the shameful way they had put his son to death, he came with all speed possible to Troy. The Achaean leaders received him coldly, but it was obvious to him who had laid the evil plot and who had aided him or tried to cover his traces. Outraged, he withdrew the force his son had once commanded and returned home to Euboea. Then he started going round the cities of Greece, calling on the absent leaders' wives and telling them their husbands were living it up in Troy with voluptuous concubines, and that when they did come back, each one of them would bring a new queen with him. When the lonely wives heard this, some went mad, some killed themselves and some even took revenge by bringing other men into their palaces. This is what Clytemnestra did, taking for a lover her husband's deadliest foe, Aegisthus, a man who hated Agamemnon bitterly for having killed his father. Harsh retribution would fall on the great Atreid the moment he returned home to Mycenae.

Before this chapter ends, we should say a few words about the custom of carrying women off as prisoners along with the booty taken in the various raids. It may seem strange today, but in those times male members of the ruling classes usually kept, in addition to their lawful wife, a number of other women who were known as concubines. This was the reason why they had so many children. However, this practice was more widespread in Africa and Asia than in Europe. Thus we see that Priam, who had nineteen children by his wife Hecabe, also had another thirty-one who were born to him out of wedlock by his concubines. In Greece there are no known cases of rulers with so many children, which means that the habit was not practised to the extent that it was known in eastern parts; nonetheless, it still existed. This is why, in the attacks the

Achaeans launched on various cities, they carried off not only loot but large numbers of pretty girls whom the leaders shared out among themselves. Yet we also see how outraged and wounded their wives were when they learned of this. Their husbands may have held that there was nothing wrong in such behaviour, but they certainly did not, which shows that the practice was not fully established in Greece, and certainly not among the ordinary people. In the Achaean camp, however, the leaders thought it perfectly natural to take concubines. The army even awarded them as prizes for acts of heroism; and we do not know what other gifts or awards would have been considered comparable to the price which Achilles set on Briseis or which Chryseis had for Agamemnon. Indeed, the lovely Briseis was the choicest gift the son of Peleus had ever been offered, the highest recognition of all his heroism and acts of valour; he would not have been deprived of her for all the world. Such were his feelings for her, and they were understood by all the camp and by the gods themselves. Much the same was true of Agamemnon, although he lacked Achilles' purity and depth of feeling. He looked on Chryseis merely as a possession, although a precious one from which he would not willingly be parted, either – but that does not mean he would not exchange her for some other gift of equal value, and that could only be some other woman of comparable beauty.

Yet why say all this'? The answer, of course, is to enable us to see those human prizes through the same eyes men looked upon them in those days. Only then will we be able to understand how right Achilles was to feel the fury that he did when his priceless gift, the lovely Briseis, was taken back from him. It seems that female beauty was destined to steal the limelight in this war. The attack on Troy was launched for lovely Helen; and now, because of the beauty of Briseis and Chryseis, heavy misfortune was to fall once more upon the Achaean camp.

This new misfortune opens a new chapter, which might be called 'The Anger of Achilles', and it is told by Homer in his 'Iliad', a long epic by the most famous poet of the ancient world and possibly of all times. Although there is no space to give the 'Iliad' in its entirety within the confines of this book, we hope to demonstrate its immortal qualities by giving the reader some of its finest passages as they stand.

HOMER'S ILIAD

Immortal muse, sing to me of the accursed anger of Achilles, son of Peleus, which brought a sea of troubles upon the Achaean army and sent the souls of many heroes down to Hades.

Thus willed the gods — that Achilles and the Atreid Agamemnon should quarrel and be foes, when the great Atreid slighted Chryses, priest of Apollo.

The priest had come from his island to the Achaean camp bearing rich gifts, for Achilles had taken his fair daughter Chryseis captive when he stormed Thebe. Now the army had given her as a gift to Agamemnon, and so the reverend priest had come before him and the other leaders, uttering these pain filled words:

"Lion-hearted Achaeans, accept these presents and give me back my precious daughter — and may the gods help you to conquer Priam's city and return victorious to your homeland."

Chryses' blessings on their venture were heard with joy, and all agreed they should accept the ransom and restore Chryseis to her father. Agamemnon, though, had no intention of giving up the lovely girl, and fixed her unhappy father with an angry glare.

"Be gone, old man!" he cried. "Do not hope to see Chryseis again. She will grow old in Mycenae. In my house she will spin and weave, and I shall have her for my companion. So get out of my sight if you want to reach home in one piece!"

Intimidated, the white-haired old man left with downcast eyes; but once he had put some distance between him and the Greeks he raised his arms up to the heavens and cried out:

"O mighty god, Apollo, protector of our island, hear my plea! If you have no complaint of me, and if your soul rejoices in the temple which I built you, if I have pleased your nostrils with the sacrifices that I offer you, then make the Danaids pay for my tears with your arrows."

Apollo gave his priest a sympathetic hearing and sped in anger to the Achaean camp with bow in hand. Standing at a distance from the ships, he began to launch his arrows in a deadly barrage, first at the animals, then at the men. It was as if a plague had struck, for the warriors dropped like flies, and for nine whole days the smoke rose to the heavens from the pyres the Achaeans lit to burn their dead companions; until finally Hera appeared before Achilles and revealed what he must do to end this scourge. Then he called an assembly of the army and told the troops:

"If war and sickness go on striking the Achaean army thus, we shall return home with our mission unaccomplished — if we escape death first, that is. Let us consult some soothsayer, then, and find out where we are to blame and why Apollo is so angry with us."

Then Calchas rose, the only one who knew all that had happened in the past, all that was happening now, and all that was to come; but he confessed he was afraid to speak lest he incur the anger of some powerful leader. Achilles managed to reassure him and finally the seer spoke out.

"Phoebus Apollo is venting his wrath on the great Atreid because he treated his priest with scorn and would not give Chryseis back. Now, to appease his rage, we must send the girl home to her father and not only forgo any thought of ransom but offer up whole herds of beasts as a rich sacrifice to the divinity."

Sparks of fury flashed from Agamemnon's eyes.

"O herald of ill-fortune," he growled between clenched teeth, "you have never had a good word for your leader, and it has always given you pleasure to warn us of catastrophe. Yes, I hold Chryses' daughter dearer than Clytemnestra herself, for she is no less in beauty, rank, knowledge and skills. But hear me, all of you: I will not refuse to give Chryseis back, for I would rather have a mighty army than one which is disintegrating. However, let someone tell me this: how am I to replace the gift with which the army honoured me? Or do you think it is fitting for the leader of the Achaeans to be left empty-handed?"

"Great Atreid," Achilles cried in anger, "you want everything but give nothing in return. Death, the great reaper, cuts us down in swathes, yet you think only of your personal interest. How can the Achaeans give you a new gift, with the best will in the world? From what I know, all those we carried off from the cities that we conquered have been shared out already, and it would not be right to take them back and share them out anew. So come to terms with it – give up the girl; and when we capture many-towered Troy you will be repaid tenfold for what you must now part with."

"You are a valiant man, Achilles," retorted Agamemnon, "and such weak attempts to trick me do not become you. The truth is that you want to keep your gift and leave me empty-handed. Well, if the Achaeans will not give me something satisfactory of their own accord, then I shall simply take the gift of any leader that I choose – and why not yours, Briseus' lovely daughter, the only one who is in all things equal to Chryseis?"

The son of Peleus turned on him with a savage glare and hissed:

"You double-crossing villain! How dare you think that you can take the prize awarded me by the whole army for my many feats of valour? And if you get away with it, don't imagine that I will go on fighting here just to do you a favour. I hold no grudge against the Trojans. They never came to make off with my flocks or steal the crops of fertile Phthia. It was for you and your brother that we came here to fight, ungrateful man – but you forget all that and even threaten that you will take away my prize. Although the heaviest burden of the fighting falls on me, you always take the lion's share of the loot and leave Achilles with the crumbs. Briseis is the one gift that I cherish, and should you steal her from me then I would a thousand times prefer to take my men and leave than stay on here to add wealth to your coffers."

"Leave, if you do not have the self-respect to fight! I shall not beg you to stay on. I have many able generals left to earn me glory and help me conquer Troy. Take your Myrmidons and go! And since you want it so, I shall be calling at your tent in person, to claim the girl you love, so that all may learn who is the leader of the Danaid host!"

Achilles was wounded to the depths of his heart. His wrath boiled over and he was about to draw his sword when at the final instant he felt a hand upon his shoulder. Turning, the hero saw Athena, visible to him alone.

"Achilles," said the goddess, "you know how much we love you, Hera and I. Resolve your disagreement by discussion, not with the sword. Curse him if you wish, and let your anger drain off that way. We see how gravely you are now being wronged, but the day will come when you will be rewarded sixfold. So listen to me, and hold back your wrath."

The hero bowed to the superior wisdom of the goddess and with a reluctant hand he pushed his sword back in its sheath. As he did so, Athena faded from his sight and Achilles' anger overflowed in words.

"You drunken, craven dog! You dare not arm yourself for battle, and all you know is how to seize the gifts of others! However, it is not your fault, but ours for keeping you as leader. Now, if I did not hold myself in check, this insult would be your last. I swear by this sceptre Zeus appointed for our most solemn oaths, there will dawn a day when all of you will come begging to Achilles on bent knee, when you fall in swathes beneath the sword of murderous Hector. Then you will bitterly regret that you did not treat the first among the Achaeans with more honour!"

Agamemnon cast a furious look upon him, but before he could open his mouth, sweet-spoken Nestor gave a reply that embodied all his long experience. The wise old man had seen two generations live and die, and now he ruled the third. Wishing with all his heart to serve the Achaeans' best interests, he rose and said:

"Alas! A grave misfortune has befallen us. Priam and his sons would all rejoice beyond imagining were they to learn that you, the greatest figures in our camp, were fixed in deadly hatred of each other. My words were heeded by renowned commanders in the good old days when I was in my prime, and you must heed them now with equal willingness. Neither should you, great-hearted Atreid, deprive Achilles of the girl the Achaeans gave him as a prize nor you, brave-spirited son of Peleus, set your will against the Great King. Born of a goddess, you may possess the greater

..."Achilles," said the goddess, "Resolve your disagreement
by discussion, not with the sword."...

strength, but he who wields Zeus' sceptre has the higher rank."

The wise old man spoke well, but they brushed aside his calm appeal to reason.

"This stripling wants to set himself above us all!" burst out Agamemnon. "And he has the insolence to curse the one it is his duty to obey."

"Don't think I'm coward enough to bend my head to all your unjust orders," Achilles interrupted. "Throw your weight around with others, not with me. Take the girl if that is what you want. You gave her to me, so you can take her back. But don't you dare take an iota more, or you'll find yourself writhing on the ground in front of the whole camp with my sword between your ribs!"

Their quarrel raged on until at last Achilles, bowing to Athena's wise advice but still wounded to the heart, withdrew to his tent.

Then Agamemnon ordered Odysseus to launch a ship with twenty oarsmen, choose his own companions, then, having driven on board a hundred beasts for a great sacrifice, to sail Chryseis back to her father's island.

Odysseus obeyed willingly, the priest's daughter went down to the ship, and as soon as it had left the shore Agamemnon summoned two of his heralds and commanded:

"Go now and bring Briseis to me. And if he does not hand her over I shall go in person with a band of warriors and take possession of her."

When the heralds got to Achilles' tent, they stood there shamefaced, afraid to open their mouths. The hero knew the cause of their discomfiture and addressed them first.

"Hail to you, heralds. Come, step closer. I know that this is not your doing. Agamemnon is to blame. Patroclus, dear friend, bring the girl out and let them take her. And may you all be witnesses to what I say: the day will come when the Achaeans cry out for my help, while I sit in my tent consumed by rage, far from the field of battle. For the Atreid does not know what he has done — and how can he who does not see the consequences of what he does today know what the next will bring? How can such a man imagine that one day the Greeks will have to fight not to take Troy but to save the ships of their own fleet!"

Holding Briseis by the hand, Patroclus led her from the tent and gave her to the heralds. With a sad look on her face, she allowed herself to be led away.

Tears welling in his eyes. Achilles rose and leaving his companions went down to the shore. Sitting on the sand, he gazed out over the sea, home of his immortal mother Thetis.

"Mother, why do the gods torment me so?" he asked. "Why, when the Fates have given me so few years to live, does Zeus let Agamemnon slight me thus? Why do you accept it, mother?" And with these words the hero burst out crying in his rage.

Thetis heard him and rose above the waves.

"Achilles, my child, why are you weeping? Tell me what is wrong."

"Everything is wrong," he answered with a sigh, "but sit down, mother, and I will tell you the whole story." Then he told her all that had happened from the time he had conquered Thebe and Lyrnessus and had taken Chryseis and Briseis prisoner, up to the point where Agamemnon had affronted him by carrying off the prize awarded as a mark of honour, the lovely daughter of Briseus. Then he added:

"Go to high Olympus, mother, and fall at Zeus' feet. He has been deeply indebted to you since the time you saved him from being caught and bound fast by the other gods. Beg him to help the Trojans till they pursue the Achaeans right down to their ships, so that the Atreid may learn how blind he was to insult the bravest of the Greeks."

The goddess' heart bled for her son. Taking him in her arms, she wiped the tears from his cheeks and stroked his auburn hair.

"It will all be done just as you ask, my son," she promised. "Stay in your tent and the day will come when the mighty Agamemnon will grovel at your feet, begging you to take pity of the Achaeans and save their skins. Just be patient. Zeus is away in Ethiopia and will be back within twelve days. The moment he returns I shall go and speak to him – and I know how to persuade him.

In the meantime, Odysseus had reached Cryses' island, given the girl back to her delighted father and brought ashore the animals, which he asked the priest to sacrifice to Phoebus as a peace offering. Chryses agreed and when the pyre was ready he stretched his arms up to the heavens and called down to Apollo.

"Silver-bowed god, protector of our island, I beg you, just as you graciously heard my former plea and afflicted the

Achaeans, listen to me now and halt the evil sickness you have sent upon them."

Apollo heard his priest and accepted the great sacrifice; and when next morning, driving by a following wind, Odysseus and his companions returned to the Achaean camp, the deadly plague of arrows had been lifted.

But the day that Thetis had been waiting for had also came. Rising from the sea, she soared up to lofty Olympus, where she found the ruler of the gods upon its highest peak. In a broken voice he told him of the injustice to her son, and Zeus was filled with sympathy. His only fear was that Hera would be angered, but he brushed this thought aside and promised to help the Trojans until such time as Achilles would be justified and his name wreathed in glory.

"And so you may be sure," he added, "that what I have promised shall be done. I bow my head before you — and whatever word I give by that submissive gesture will not be taken back."

As Zeus lowered his immortal head, the heavens were rent asunder and Olympus shook to its foundations. The promise he had made was now irrevocable.

Pleased with the outcome of her mission, Thetis returned to the blue depths of the sea. Hera, however, had followed the whole scene and was indeed enraged. Zeus knew the time had come to put her in her place.

"Do not expect me to reveal my deepest thoughts to you," he warned. "Things which no god should know will not be revealed to you either, even if you are my wife. All I can promise is that when something must be heard by all, then you will be the first to learn it."

All night the ruler of the gods lay sleepless, racking his brain to find a way to heap glory on Achilles and inflict heavy losses on the Achaeans. Finally he called for Oneirus, god of dreams, and told him:

"Deceiving Oneirus, run and seek out Agamemnon where he sleeps, and turn his dreaming head with a false message that the gods agree to give victory to him and wreak destruction on the Trojans."

Oneirus sped through the night and appeared before Agamemnon in the shape of Nestor, the wise old man the son of Atreus held such in high esteem.

"Awake, great Atreid," he whispered in his ear, "when a ruler holds the fate of nations in his hands there are times that he cannot afford to sleep. Arise! I am sent by Zeus to tell you all the gods have agreed to award the great victory to our side. The time has come for the final assault upon Troy."

Agamemnon sprang awake, filled with fierce joy. In his delusion he imagined he would conquer towered Troy that very day, while the truth was that Zeus had many sorrows in store for the Danaids and their Trojan foes alike.

He quickly dressed, woke up his heralds and commanded them to rouse the leaders and summon them to conference.

They all met by Nestor's ship and listened in astonishment as Agamemnon told them of his dream.

"But first I want to put the army to the test," he said in closing. "I shall summon them and say that we are setting sail for home. Hold them in check, if need be, when they hear the news. We must find out what appetite they have for battle."

All the kings agreed and each one hurried off to muster up his forces.

Like bees the Argive multitude swarmed from their tents and clambered from the ships. When they were all assembled, nine heralds bellowed for silence, that the Great King might be heard. When finally the milling crowd below grew quiet, Agamemnon rose and said:

"Achaean heroes, warriors of Ares, Zeus has misled me cruelly. He promised Troy to me – yet we have fought now for so many years and the war's end is nowhere in sight. The Trojans may be few in number on their own, but allies skilled in the arts of war have flocked to their side and prevented me from taking haughty Troy. Nine years have passed. Our ships have rotted on the shore and sun and wind have torn their sails to shreds. Years now our lonely wives have waited for us and our children longed to see our faces, yet we have not achieved what we set out to do. The gods do not want us to topple Ilium's lofty ramparts, and now there is no choice but to go back to the lands that gave us birth. That is all, then; we leave for home."

The listening army stirred like a sea whipped into storm. A roar of joy rose to the heavens, and they all began a mad stampede towards the ships, raising the dust in clouds. Men pushed and shoved and were trampled underfoot in their haste to drag the fleet down to the water, crazed with delight to be returning to their beloved homeland. Or so

they thought, for the poor deluded fools did not know of
the son of Atreus' secret plan.

So desperate was the soldiers' longing to be gone, it now
became very difficult to hold the heaving masses back. Had
Athena not sped to warn Odysseus, the Trojan war would
have come to a hasty end that day. But Odysseus moved
fast to rally the remaining leaders and by their concerted
efforts they succeeded in keeping the troops in check.

There was one, however, who voiced loud complaints
and would not listen to his commanders. This was Thersites, an ugly, hunch-backed soldier with a limp who had a
habit of speaking out unpleasant truths.

"What drives you, Atreid, to torture us like this?" he
cried. "What more do you want — women? You have as
many as you could desire, the ones we bring you, of course,
whenever we have stormed some city. Gold is it that you
lack, then? No, some father always lays it at your feet in his
anxiety to get back his son — the son we brought to you,
bound hand and foot. And what reward do we get for all of
this? Nothing but cruel deception! Achaeans, cringing
cowards, why do you fear this man? Come on, fellows,
let's get out of here! We've had our fill of fighting in these
parts. Let him stay here alone and sit upon his treasures.
Then, mighty Agamemnon, you will learn how much you
undervalued all our efforts. And as if your contempt for us
were not enough, you had the effrontery to insult a man
more valiant than you by far and take away the gift of
honour awarded him by the whole army. I tell you, Atreid,
if Achilles had not put his sword back in its sheath, that

..."What drives you, Atreid, to torture us like this?"...

insult would have been the last you ever committed!"

"Hold your peace, Thersites!" Odysseus retorted. "you've got a smooth tongue in your head but you're the last one here who has a right to criticize. If there's a worse man here than you, then show him to me!" He went on in the same harsh vein and ended by striking him with the sceptre. Shrinking from the blow in fear, Thersites wiped the tears from his eyes with the back of his hand. Only a few minutes earlier, many had admired the bold way he had spoken out, but now the admiration turned to jeers and catcalls as he slunk off muttering protests under his breath.

Then Odysseus addressed the crowd. He knew exactly what to say.

"I do not blame you for wanting to go home," he told them. "Who doesn't want to? If a man is separated from his folks for just a month he longs to be with them again. And we've been here for nine years. Tell me this, though: would it not be a shame to return home empty-handed after such a time? Be patient a little longer, friends, and let us see if Calchas' words prove true. All of you must remember, back there at Aulis – it seems like yesterday to me – when we saw the snake swallow the nine fledgling sparrows and then turn to stone. Nine years Calchas told us we would fight, but on the tenth we would seize Troy and her wealth. So far, everything has come about as prophesied. Let us remain here then, brave-souled Achaeans, till we have captured Priam's mighty city!"

A roar of expectation rose from the massed troops; such was the power of Odysseus' words to please! Then other leaders spoke, including Nestor and finally Agamemnon. The army steadily grew more enthusiastic, helped on by Athena who walked unseen among the warriors filling their souls with resolution until all those who but a little while before had rushed headlong for the ships were now more eager to do battle than set eyes on their dear homeland.

Then Agamemnon sacrificed a fattened five-year-old ox to Zeus. By his side stood his brother Menelaus, Nestor of Pylos, and Idomeneus from Crete. There too were Diomedes, Odysseus and the two Ajaxes. All of them filled their hands with barley to make the invocation. When this was done, their commander raised his arms and cried:

"Almighty Zeus, son of Cronus, accept this sacrifice and give me the power to burn down Priam's palace with my fire. Give my spear the strength to pierce the breast of Hector and throw countless Trojans lifeless in the dust before the sun goes down!"

Zeus took the sacrifice but did not heed his words. The lord of gods and men wanted a hard-fought struggle on that day.

Soon the plain was swarming with the Argive forces. The whole army was there, set out in formation, each phalanx headed by a general. Mighty Agamemnon stood out in their midst with his tall stature and his shining armour. In features he resembled Zeus, his waist and sturdy thighs recalled the war-god Ares, while his rippling chest was like that of powerful Poseidon. Just as a bull looms proudly out among the herd, so the great Atreid could be distinguished among his gallant host.

Yet while the Achaeans were preparing to give battle, the Trojans, too, were getting ready for the fight. Zeus had sent Iris winging on her way to give them warning. The news that Achilles had withdrawn in anger to his tent had given them fresh courage, and they had decided to come out from behind the walls and strike the Danaids upon the open plain. Without delay, they drew their forces up beneath the city's towering walls.

Though Hector commanded all the Trojan units, this day Paris took his place at the army's head, in search of glory. Fair as a god and wearing gleaming armour, he stood there proud and restless to begin, his sword tucked in his waist and a bow slung over one shoulder. Determined to fight it out until the death, he took a few steps forward and brandishing two spears on high he roared with all the power in his lungs:

"Valiant Achaeans! Let the battle begin, and may Zeus bestow the victory on the side he favours!"

Immediately, both sides advanced. With eager step and savage war-cries the Achaeans and the Trojans drew together. Suddenly Menelaus spied Paris at the head of the enemy troops and he sprang forward to meet him face to face. Like a hungry lion that sees a well-fed deer and leaps to tear it into pieces, he flung himself upon his adulterous foe.

The moment Paris saw him, his warlike pride dissolved into thin air. All his courage failed him and he looked desperately for a place to hide. 'Safety in numbers!' he thought, and in his fear he ran and hid himself among the

Trojan ranks. His brother Hector pursued him in disgust and the moment he caught up with him began to hurl insults in his face:

"You cheating womanizer!" he screamed, "You strutting coward! If we of Troy had had the sense we should have skinned you alive when you abducted the fair Helen and brought her here. What you did was an insult to a race of heroes!"

Paris bent his head in shame.

"You have every right to speak to me this way," he answered. "I know my courage failed me, but I am afraid no longer. Listen to me and I shall prove it to you. Step out before the armies and shout these words to the Danaids and the Trojans: 'Paris demands that both sides lay down their arms so that Menelaus and he can fight it out between them. Whoever wins will take Helen and all the treasure with her and the opposing forces will swear to part in peace. Thus this long war will at last come to its end and we shall enjoy the fruits of fertile Troy and they the fair land of Greece and its lovely maidens."

Hector was pleased with his brother's proposal and so he stepped out between the armies and shouted it to both the Achaeans and Trojans. There was surprise on either side but all were happy to accept. Then Menelaus came forward saying:

"At last the day has come when we can end this war. Let us pit our skills in single combat, so that our two peoples can part in friendship, and may Zeus choose which one of us is to die. All I ask is that you first bring a white ram to sacrifice to Helius and we another to offer up to Zeus. And let the reverend Priam come in person for the rites, rather than some son of his. Young people's minds are easily turned from their purpose while older men, with all their yesterdays, can see tomorrow's consequences clearer and guard themselves against the evil hour."

Thus spoke Menelaus and his foresight met with universal applause.

From the tower above the Scaean Gates, Priam, Antenor and the city elders had been watching with puzzled eyes. Warned by the goddess Iris, Helen, too, came to the tower. The moment she appeared, all were dazzled by her beauty and the elders said: "The Achaeans are right, but then so are the Trojans, to fight so many years over such a lovely creature." However, one of them added: "Lovely though she may be, it is better she go back where she came from rather than ruin fall upon us and our children."

While they were talking, Priam called Helen to his side.

"Come, daughter, and look upon your first husband, your relatives and all those you once knew. I place no blame on you for what has happened; it is the gods who are responsible. It was they who wished to see this thrice-accursed war. But tell me, who is that Achaean down there? How tall he is, how handsome and imposing! He has the majesty of a true king."

"I am grateful for your kind words, dear father-in-law," Helen replied, "but I am to blame, and heavily, whatever you may say. I should have chosen death over dishonour all those years ago, and yet I followed Paris. It was the wrong

..."Come, daughter, and look upon your first husband,
your relatives and all those you once knew."...

path that I chose, and now that I think of the daughter that I left, I melt in tears and wish that I had never been born, bitch that I am! As for the man you asked me of, that is mighty Agamemnon, son of Atreus, a valiant warrior and brother of Menelaus, my first husband."

Priam looked on his foe with admiration.

"Thrice-happy Atreid!" he exclaimed. "A king like you, in command of such a countless host, I never saw before. But tell me, child, who is that one with the broad chest, who marches to and fro among his men like a thick-curled ram among the flock?"

"That is Odysseus of Ithaca. There is no cleverer or more cunning man alive than he."

"A formidable brain, Odysseus has," Antenor added. "I got to know him when I offered him hospitality in my home. Granted he doesn't make a good impression at first sight. He stands before you with his head bent down and you take him for a fool or churlish fellow. But when that mighty voice of his bursts from his chest, the words he utters, cool and clear as snowflakes, immediately dispel the bad impression, and all you feel is admiration for the keenness of his mind."

"And that one there," asked Priam a third time, "he who surpasses all of them in height and breadth of shoulder, who is he?"

"That is great Ajax, the fortress of the Achaeans," Helen replied. "Next to him is Idomeneus, the leader of the Cretans; but I cannot see my brothers Castor and Polydeuces anywhere, and I fear some harm may have befallen them and they did not come with the other Greeks to Troy."

There were many more whom Priam wished to ask about, but he was cut short by Idaeus, who had been sent by Hector.

"Rise, son of Laomedon," he told him. "The Trojans are asking for you. The war is coming to an end. Paris will fight Menelaus in single combat and whoever wins will take Helen and the treasure, while all of us will seal a pact of peace."

When he heard that his son would fight Menelaus, a shudder ran through Priam. This was dreadful news. But, he ordered the grooms to harness the horses, and climbed into the royal chariot with Antenor. They came out through the Scaean Gates and soon arrived at the place of sacrifice, where all was ready. Once Priam was in place, Agamemnon called upon the gods:

"O father Zeus, glorious and great, who looks down on us from mount Ida, and you, Sun, you who see all from the heavens, and Rivers and Earth, and you, immortal Gods, who vent harsh punishment on those who break their vows – accept this oath: if Paris should kill Menelaus, he will keep Helen and all the treasure, and we shall leave for home. And if Menelaus slays Paris, the Trojans will give Helen back with all the treasures and in addition such a fine as will be remembered by generations yet to come. But if the Trojans go back on their word after the death of Paris, we shall stay here till we have won by war that which is ours by right."

The oath sworn, he slew the two rams with his pitiless knife while Achaeans and Trojans poured wine upon the ground, crying out:

"Just as this red wine trickles to the earth, so will the blood of those who break their vow be shed!"

Then Priam said in a voice which trembled with emotion:

"Only the gods know which of these two will win and which will die. As for me, I cannot bear to see my dear son wager his life in such a contest. I shall withdraw into the city."

As soon as Priam had left, Odysseus and Hector made two lots and dropped them into a bronze helmet to be shaken and thus decide who would first cast his deadly spear. Meanwhile, the troops of both sides crowded round and cried out in one voice:

"O father Zeus, punish the one who bears the heavier load of guilt and kindled this enmity between us. Send him to Hades first, then let the friendship of our two peoples be sealed with vows of love."

Hector shook the lots and luck favoured Paris. The son of Priam stepped forward boldly, and Menelaus did the same. They paced the distance out between the opponents, who took up their positions. With bated breath the crowd watched the two heroes, whose savage expressions revealed the depth of the hatred which divided them.

Paris flung his spear. It fell with force upon the stout shield of the king of Sparta, but its bronze tip bent and did not pierce it through. Now came Menelaus' turn. "Great

Zeus," he cried, "make this blow snuff out the life of the one who played so foully with me, that now and for all time no other man may dare to abuse such hospitality as I showed him!" This said, he launched his spear with terrifying strength. It pierced the shield and sliced through Paris' tunic, but he ducked in time to avoid death by a hairsbreadth. Then Menelaus charged down on him, sword in hand, and struck him a great blow upon the helmet; but the sword-blade snapped and he flung it from him in disgust.

"You are unjust to me, father Zeus," he muttered. "My spear-shot went for nothing, my sword is shattered – and still I have not killed him."

This did not mean Menelaus had lost hope. He flung himself on Paris, seized the horsehair tuft that crowned his helmet, and pulling hard on it he threw him to the ground and began to drag him by the head. So tightly did the helmet-strap press down on Paris' neck he would have throttled him had Aphrodite not run up at the last moment, cut the noose and saved his life. The Atreid was left with the empty helmet in his hands, which he tossed spinning through the air to land among his comrades. And while they held it high and showed it to the crowds, he threw himself upon his Trojan foe once more to tear him limb from limb. Yet once more the goddess rescued Paris, wrapping him in a cloud, while Menelaus, who did not realize he had lost his quarry, searched like a ravening beast among the Trojans to find the man that none of them would have hidden anyway because they all hated him worse than death itself.

Finally great Agamemnon stepped out before the crowd and cried:

"Trojans, Dardanians and your other allies, listen to me. We all saw who the winner was, so give us back fair Helen and the treasure, together with the tribute we agreed upon, then let us all rejoice that peace has come."

The Achaeans shouted their agreement.

Yet high on Olympus Hera was watching in anxiety, lest peace indeed be declared and Troy saved from destruction.

"What has the city done to merit all this hatred?" Zeus enquired. "Were you to swallow Priam, his sons and all the men of Troy alive, still your appetite for vengeance would not be satisfied. However, do as you see fit – but never let me hear a whisper of complaint if ever I decide to destroy some city that you love."

"There are three cities I am fond of: Sparta, Argos and Mycenae. Burn them all to ashes if their people ever anger you – but let me raze Ilium to its foundations."

Then Zeus sent Athena to mingle with the Trojans and egg them on to go back on their oath, so that the fighting might begin once more.

Athena, who wanted to see Troy's ruin as much as Hera did, ran gleefully to the Trojan camp in search of a fine marksman, Pandarus son of Lycaon, whose bow had been given to him by Apollo himself. On finding him she took the shape of one of Antenor's sons, went up to him and said:

"Would you dare shoot an arrow at Menelaus? Think of the glory for you if you killed him, and what honours Paris would heap upon your head. Don't think about it twice, then — just promise Apollo a great sacrifice when you return home after the war's end."

The fool was soon persuaded. Making his bargain with Apollo, he took up his bow and, hidden behind the shields of his companions, took aim at the renowned hero. Nor did he miss his mark. The arrow caught Menelaus in the belt, passed through it, pierced his breastplate, too; and had Athena not been watching over him and slowed the arrow down, the son of Atreus would have been killed. Even so, he was badly hurt and blood gushed forth from the wound.

That was it. An arrow had changed everything. The solemn oath had been flouted and the nine years' war which had brought such long and terrible suffering to Achaeans and Trojans alike was destined to go on and heap far worse upon them.

The fighting soon flared up. The Danaid ranks surged forward like the angry sea. With fierce cries the Trojans lunged in, too. Athena was there to aid the Greeks, while bloodthirsty Ares was helping on the Trojan side. Both gods and men were locked in combat. Demos and Phobus, Ares' two sons, were on the battlefield as well, spreading panic in their path. So was his sister, Eris, who darted hither and thither, invisible, like a maddened creature, feeding the flames of war.

The leaders were the first to plunge into the thick of battle: Agamemnon, Ajax, Odysseus, Diomedes, Menelaus and Idomeneus. The mighty Ajax, who was descended from Zeus, smote Simoeisius, who fell like a tall tree

beneath the axe, in the flower of his youth. As he was stripping him of his weapons, Antiphus, son of Priam, flung a spear at him; but instead of hitting Ajax it struck Odysseus' friend, Leucus, who was dragging the body away. He fell dead upon the corpse and thus a Greek and a Trojan were locked in lifeless embrace. Beside himself with grief and rage at the loss of his companion, Odysseus hurled himself upon the Trojans. Transfixing Priam's bastard son Democoön with his spear he robbed him of his life. Cowed by the fury of his attack, the Trojan forces wavered and fell back. With yells of triumph the Achaeans surged forward, pulling the dead back to the rear; but Apollo, who could see it all, cried out in a loud voice:

"Do not retreat before the Achaeans, men of Troy. Their

bodies are not made of stone or iron. They are not proof against the bronze that tears the flesh; and Achilles, still gripped by his rage, does not fight but still sits idle by the ships."

Heeding the god's words, the Trojans took fresh courage and put up a heroic resistance. First Peirous, the leader of the Thracians, struck at Diores, the Epeian chief, and laid him lifeless on the ground; but before he could savour his victory, Thoas of Aetolia killed him in his turn. He would have stripped him of his weapons, too, but brave as he was, he dared not pit himself against such numbers, for many Thracians were standing guard upon the spot where their dead leader lay.

Many of the Achaeans won renown in this great battle,

yet one stood out above all others. This was Diomedes, son of the illustrious Tydeus. The goddess Athena wished to give him the greatest glory on this day.

When the rash Pandarus saw the havoc Diomedes was wreaking upon the Trojans, he ran forward without hesitation. Although he had not succeeded in killing Menelaus, he believed that now his chance had come to win greater glory still by dispatching the fearsome son of Tydeus. Without a moment's hesitation he stretched his dreaded bow to its full limit and loosed the pointed shaft. It caught Diomedes in the shoulder.

"Look, Trojan heroes!" he cried out in triumph. "I have hit the bravest of the Achaeans. Come, see where he falls!"

But Diomedes did not fall. Sthenelus, his charioteer, drew out the arrow while he called on Athena to aid him.

In an instant, the goddess was at his side.

"Fight on, Diomedes!" she urged. "I have breathed into your heart all the strength and daring of your father Tydeus. Fear no one. Even if you see Aphrodite come before you, strike at her, too."

Diomedes sprang into battle once again, and woe to those who crossed his path. Two sons of Priam, Echemon and Chromius, ran to cut off his advance but he slew them both and took their arms and horses.

Now he cast about for Pandarus and saw him coming on his chariot, accompanied by Aeneas, the son of Anchises and Aphrodite.

Sthenelus' heart quailed when he saw them.

"They are invincible," he gulped. "we must get out of

here!"

"You know I never turn my back upon the enemy," Diomedes replied. "You stay in the chariot and I will fight on foot; and if Athena should give me the victory, run to seize Aeneas' horses – they were born of the immortal steeds which Zeus gave to Tros when he carried his son Ganymedes off to Olympus. A fairer youth was never born into this world. Zeus has him now to hand round nectar to the gods at their symposia."

With these words he jumped down from the chariot and ran to meet his foes.

"Son of mighty Tydeus," Pandarus called out to him, "I see that though I wounded you, you have escaped death's clutches. This time, I shall send you down to Hades, mark my words!" A second later he hurled his long spear at the hero. It tore through his shield but was stopped short by his breastplate.

"I have wounded you again!" Pandarus cried out in a loud voice that all around could hear.

"Wrong!" retorted Diomedes. "You did not even scratch me. But I shall not rest quiet until I have sated Ares with your blood." And he flung his heavy spear in turn. With the aid of Athena it found its mark: Pandarus toppled lifeless from his chariot, while the horses reared in terror.

Then Aeneas leapt down from the traces and brandishing his shield and spear he angrily dared the enemy to approach the corpse – for he feared the Argives would drag it off and treat it with dishonour. Diomedes, however, snatching up a stone which two men of our times would have difficulty in lifting, flung it at Aeneas and broke his leg.

The son of Aphrodite fell heavily, tried to raise himself upon his hands but fainted with the pain and would have drifted off into the dark night of death if his immortal mother had not hastened to carry him from the field of battle. Nothing could restrain Diomedes by now. He loosed his spear at Aphrodite, too, as she was carrying her unconscious son, and wounded her in the forearm. Her immortal blood began to gush out from the cut and with loud cries of pain she let Aeneas fall to earth again and flew up terror-stricken to Olympus to complain to Zeus.

"My daughter," Zeus replied, "the works of war are not for such as you. You were made for the arts of love. Leave the rest to Athena and that mad dog Ares."

When the bleeding Aphrodite let Aeneas fall, Apollo sped to save him, but Diomedes did not hesitate to threaten him as well, so intent was he on dealing the death-blow to his enemy and carrying off his splendid armour.

"Son of Tydeus," roared the archer-god in rage, "do not presume to think that we of Olympus can be compared to you mere mortals. Watch your step, I say, and move aside."

Diomedes obeyed the god and withdrew while Apollo took Aeneas in his arms and flew up to the acropolis of Troy, where, with the help of the gods, he soon became well again. But as for the wonderful horses, they were led off to the Achaean ships by Sthenelus.

Uneasy at what had happened, Apollo returned to the battle, where he encountered the fearsome god of war.

"Ares," he told him, "do you see what this son of Tydeus

is doing to us? First he wounds Aphrodite, and now he threatens me with violence. He's gone so berserk that he'd take on father Zeus himself. It's time we saw to it his fighting days were over."

Ares at once inspired the Trojans with fresh zeal and courage, then ran to fetch Hector and the renowned Sarpedon, king of Lycia, who was a son of Zeus. As he pushed his way into the front ranks of the fighting, the situation changed in a flash. The mere sight of these three fearsome warriors was enough to make the Achaeans fall back. One alone scorned the danger to his life and held his ground, Tlepolemus, the son of Heracles. Sarpedon stepped out to challenge him – and thus a grandson and a son of Zeus stood face to face in deadly combat. They hurled their spears at the same instant. Tlepolemus hit Sarpedon in the leg, but the latter's spear-thrust caught him in the heart and flung him to the ground.

When Odysseus saw the death of Heracles' son his heart was filled with pain and rage. Hurling himself upon the Lycian hordes he killed seven of Sarpedon's companions unaided and would have slain many more had not Hector stepped out before him accompanied by none other than Ares. Six heroes fell at once beneath the fearsome lance of the Trojan leader and once again the situation became critical for the Achaeans. At this juncture, Hera anxiously petitioned to have Ares taken out of the fighting. Zeus not only agreed but advised her to use Athena for the purpose. She carried out her mission well: under her guidance

Diomedes managed to inflict a humiliating wound upon the war-god, who left the field a sorry spectacle and seething with resentment. He soon reached Olympus and ran at once to his father to complain!

"Serves you right," replied Zeus. "Of all the gods on Olympus, you're the most hateful. You love nothing but enmity, war and blood. If you weren't my son, I'd have thrown you from Olympus into the depths of Tartarus where you would long forever for a ray of light in the eternal darkness. Now, go and get your wound bound up and try to act a little more sensibly."

As soon as his wound was healed, he ran furiously back onto the battlefield searching for Athena.

"I'll teach you, she-dog!" he cried on catching sight of the goddess; and with that he hurled his lance straight at her with brutal force. But Athena jumped nimbly aside and the lance sailed past. With one quick movement she snatched up a great stone, hurled it at Ares and hit him square in the throat.

"Aagh!" A strangled gasp escaped Ares' lips as he tottered and fell headlong, covering seven whole fields with his body. To his aid ran Aphrodite, but the daughter of Zeus immediately struck her across the chest with her heavy hand. So hard was the blow that the eyes of the goddess of love clouded over and she, too, fell unconscious at Ares' side. Now the pair of them lay beaten and humiliated in the dust.

"If all who help the Trojans were like you, this war would have ended long ago," said Athena in a mocking voice, leaving them stretched out upon the silent earth.

Fired by his latest feat, the son of Tydeus now turned upon the Lycian forces. One of their number, bolder than the rest, came forth to challenge the great hero. When Diomedes saw him he stopped short, amazed by his daring and good looks. He was as handsome as a god.

"Who are you, bold warrior?" he enquired.

The other stood his ground and answered with cool courage:

"Worthy son of Tydeus, my name is Glaucus and my father is Hippolochus, son of the hero Bellerophon. I was born in Lycia, but my family has its roots in Corinth."

And having recounted how his grandfather Bellerophon had come to Lycia, he added:

"When my father sent me here to fight, he told me always to stand in the front ranks and with my bravery do honour to the generations of my family who won renown in Corinth and on Lycia's broad plains. I am proud to be descended from such a race."

Diomedes was astonished by his words.

"But you are old friends of my family," he exclaimed. "My grandfather Oeneus gave hospitality to Bellerophon for twenty days, and on his parting they exchanged rich gifts. If ever you should come to Argos, I, too, shall be delighted to receive you in my turn, and I know that you will do the same for me if my travels take me to Lycia. There is no cause for us two to fight. There are Trojans in plenty for me to kill, and as many Achaeans for you. Come, let us exchange our weapons and our armour, so that all the world may know that we are friends from generations back."

The two of them immediately jumped down from their chariots, exchanged their fighting gear, and with a handshake sealed a vow of brotherly affection.

Meanwhile, Hector was growing increasingly resentful that all the Trojans should be fighting except for Paris, the one man responsible for all their woes – and so he hurried back into the city to seek him out.

Passing through the Scaean Gates he was stopped by the mothers and daughters of his warriors, anxious for news of their kin. He had an answer for each one of them. The fears of many he was able to relieve, but for others there were bitter tears.

Hector now went up to the palace, where the first person he encountered was his mother, Hecabe. Clinging to his hand, she poured out her anxiety and offered him some wine.

"It is not proper, mother. I cannot drink unwashed or offer a libation up to Zeus – and nor should I delay. But you women, go to the temple of Athena and offer her a sacrifice in the hope she may take pity on this holy city. I must run to find Paris and bring him back to the battle. That is, if he will listen to me, curse him. Zeus must have saved the fellow especially for our destruction. If only I could see him sink into the depths of Hades, then all my sorrows would be lifted from me."

With heavy hearts, mother and son went their separate ways. Hecabe called her women to her, and, as Hector had advised, they went to placate the goddess with their gifts. All was in vain, however, for Athena would not accept the offerings.

Hector found Paris with Helen surrounded by a crowd of female slaves.

"Miserable creature!" Hector cried when he beheld this scene. "The flower of Troy's youth is being killed for you. Get up at once, before our homes are wrapped in flames!"

"I am coming," Paris answered. "You have every right to be angry with me. I was in great pain before and could not come. But now I am ready. Let me just put on my armour and I will be with you in a moment. Go on ahead and I will catch up with you."

"Brother-in-law," said Helen then to Hector, "I am ashamed to look you in the face. It would have been a thousand times better if my mother had thrown me in the sea at birth or abandoned me on some wild mountain-side rather than have this evil destiny befall us all. Sit down awhile and rest, though, for you are fighting a hard struggle on account of my faithlessness and Paris' adultery. Yet this was what Zeus willed our fate to be, so that we might go down in song and story."

"Thank you, Helen, but I cannot stay. The Trojan forces are calling for me. All I wish is to see my beloved wife and new-born son for a few moments, for I do not know if I shall ever set eyes on them again."

But the lovely Andromache was not in the palace. Filled with anxiety on hearing that the Trojan forces were pulling back, she had hastened to the Scaean Gates to glean further news.

With long strides, Hector hurried down the city's streets. He no longer had any hopes of seeing Andromache, and passing once more through the Scaean Gates he was already marching out to battle.

"Oh, Hector, are you mad? Where are you going?" came that familiar voice from behind him; and turning his head he saw her standing there, his incomparable wife, and at her side the nursemaid, with young Astyanax in her arms. A smile lit Hector's weary face when he set eyes on them. With tears upon her cheeks, Andromache pressed herself against him, and placing both her hands in his broad palm she said:

"Your impetuosity will be the death of you. Take pity on our child, you fool, and on me, who will be left a widow, for soon the Achaeans will throw themselves upon you as one man and that will be the end of you. Yet if I am to lose you, a thousand times better that I descend to Hades than go on living with my pain. I have no one left in this world. My father died by the sword of Achilles, as did all my brothers; and my mother, after first tasting the bitterness of slavery, was killed by Artemis in her rage. Hector, you are father, mother and brother to me as well as my beloved companion. Have pity on us and stay here in the fortress; do not make a widow of me and our child an orphan. Just place our forces near the wild fig-tree, where the wall is easiest to scale and the Argives have three times tried to break into the city."

"I have thought all these things over, my dear one," Hector replied, "but I cannot leave the battle. How could I face my men were I to do so, or look their mothers in the eye? To show myself a coward is more than my heart could bear. I have learned to be always in the front rank, earning glory for my father and myself. And yet I know the day will dawn when our sacred city will be lost and with it Priam and all our people. Even so, it is not so much the anguish of the Trojans that distresses me, nor king Priam and my respected mother, nor my any courageous brothers who may roll dead in the dirt; no, none of these burns my soul so much as the thought of your disgrace when some helmeted Achaean drags you behind him as his slave, while you weep bitter tears. If only you could know the hurt it gives me to think of the pain that will weigh upon your heart when you bend enslaved over some loom in distant Argos, or stagger under the pitcher's weight bringing water from the well. If only you knew how much it tortures me to think that men may look into your tear-filled eyes and say: 'There is the wife of Hector, the greatest warlord of the Trojans!' And then you will feel fresh pain at the loss of the one man who could have saved you. But may Zeus make the earth lie heavy on my grave, so that your wailing will not reach my ears as you are dragged away."

With these words, Hector held his arms out to his son Astyanax. But the little boy was frightened by the glint of his bronze armour and the bristling horsehair on his helmet and cowered back. Both Andromache and her husband laughed at this, and Hector took his polished helmet off and laid it on the ground. Then he took up his son and kissed him, dandled him in his arms and finally said:

"O father Zeus, let my son be as I was, first among the Trojans, to rule with honour over a powerful Ilium! O gods, grant that his mother's heart may lift in joy when she sees him returning victorious from battle with rich booty, and may she be more joyful still when she hears men say: 'His father was a mighty man, but he is even finer.'"

Having said this, he placed the baby in its mother's fragrant arms and she, smiling through her tears, bent forward to receive his caress and parting words.

"If I have hurt you I did not mean to do so. No one can know what his end will be," he said, putting on his helmet once again. "Neither the brave man nor the coward can escape his fate."

Hector left – and that was their last farewell.

As he walked out beyond the walls, Paris caught him up. He, too, was determined to fight bravely. Both men flung themselves into the thick of battle and fired the Trojans with renewed enthusiasm. Then Hector decided to engage one of the Achaeans in single combat. It was his brother Helenus who gave him the idea, and seer that he was, he told him that his time had not yet come to be killed.

"I have thought all these things over, my dear one,
but I cannot leave the battle."...

Holding his long spear like a barrier, Hector used it to push the Trojans back and stop the fighting. Seeing this action from the other side, Agamemnon did likewise. Then Hector stepped forward and cried out:

"Trojans and Achaeans, listen to the words that my heart speaks to me. I wish to fight with an Achaean hero, with anyone who has the spirit for it. Let Zeus be witness to what I shall say next. If my opponent should defeat me, he may take my weapons, but my body he must give back to my own people, to be buried with honours. And if I should be the one to deal the death-blow, then I will take his weapons and the Danaids may bury him on the tip of the Hellespont and raise a tall mound over his grave so that he may be remembered by future generations. Then seamen sailing in those waters will say: 'That is the tomb of a hero who died long ago. He was killed by the great Hector, although he put up a brave fight.'"

At the bold Trojan's words a deadly silence fell upon the Achaean camp. Nobody said a word. They were ashamed to decline the challenge, but afraid to accept it. When the hush became too uncomfortable to bear, Menelaus rose in indignation, shouting and cursing. After calling them all boastful cowards and lily-livered maidens, he concluded, his heart heavy with foreboding:

"Since none of you dares stand up to Hector, I will fight the duel with him myself – and may the gods give victory to whom they please!"

Noble Menelaus, as you spoke those words you must have seen your own death written on the wall, for you knew that you were far outmatched by Hector.

"But you are mad!" Agamemnon immediately retorted. "How can you fight a hero that even Achilles is afraid of? Stand aside; the Achaeans will find someone who is a match for him."

Menelaus obeyed his leader's orders; then white-haired Nestor tottered to his feet and said:

"Old Peleus would groan from deep within his heart and beg to be dragged down to Hades rather than see the sons of the Achaeans go numb with fear before the Trojan Hector. O father Zeus and Athena and Apollo, did I but have my youth, as I had it then when we of Pylos fought against the Arcadians and in their foremost rank stood Ereuthalion, a very god in strength and stature, whom all trembled at the sight of. He, too, challenged the boldest of us to match himself against him and then as now, no one rose to the challenge. So I took him on, youngest in the army as I was, and Athena accorded me the victory. Tall as an oak, broad as a barn he may have been, the great Ereuthalion, but I laid him flat out on the ground. I never killed a braver or a stronger man. Ah, if only I could have my youth back, then Hector would find himself with somebody to fight! But now, shame on us all, no one dares to come out and face him."

The old man's scorn worked to some effect, for at once nine warriors leapt to their feet together: Agamemnon, Diomedes, the two Ajaxes, Idomeneus, Meriones, Odysseus, Eurypylus and Thoas. Now they were all so eager to fight the unmatchable Hector that in the end they were obliged to draw for the privilege. The lot fell to the giant-like Ajax, son of Telamon. He stepped forward immediately, armed to the teeth, a smile of anticipation lighting up his bloodthirsty face. The Achaeans saw him and rejoiced. The Trojans saw him and were seized by fear. Even the great Hector felt his heart beat faster at the sight of him, but he stood firm.

A moment later they were face to face and began to throw down challenges. Ajax first attempted to intimidate his opponent, but seeing that Hector was not to be cowed he behaved towards him with more chivalry, offering to let him have first spear-throw. In response, the valiant Trojan promised he would not use foul play.

Hector hurled his spear. It stuck quivering in Ajax' towering shield but did not pierce it through. Next Ajax made his throw; his spear tore clean through Hector's great round shield, but ducking quickly he avoided death. Retrieving their weapons, they both threw again, but this time the bronze point of Hector's lance bent on the metal lining Ajax' shield, while the latter's blade grazed Hector's neck. Ignoring the blood which spurted out, he picked up a great stone and cast it with great force at Ajax. It hit his shield but without result. Then the son of Telamon heaved up a boulder bigger still, one the size of a mill-stone, and sent it spinning into Hector's shield. So huge was its mass and speed that it flung him flat upon his back; but Apollo, who was following the combat, slipped in unseen and raised him to his feet. The two heroes had just drawn their swords when the heralds Talthybius and Idaeus stepped between them, holding up their rods of office.

"Stop!" cried Idaeus, Priam's spokesman. "The fight has shown Zeus loves you both. Dusk is falling and we must obey the dictates of the night."

The combat was at an end. The two opponents sheathed their swords and shook each other by the hand.

"Now let us exchange gifts," declared Hector, "so that men will say of us: 'These two engaged in mortal combat and yet they parted friends.'"

And with these words he presented Ajax a sword with silver chasing and was given a belt of royal purple in return.

The duel between the two heroes may have ended on this note of friendship, but everyone knew the battle would be renewed next day in all its savagery.

That night, the leaders of the Achaeans met for a war-council. On Nestor's suggestion, they agreed to work through the hours of darkness to build a protective earth-work around their camp and the beached ships.

The Trojans met in council, too. They were addressed by old Antenor, whom they all respected.

"Trojans and Dardanians," he told them, "what I have to say comes from the depths of my heart, and you must pay heed to me. Fair Helen and all the treasure must be re-turned. Now we are fighting in defiance of our oaths, we cannot expect the gods to give us victory."

Paris sprang to his feet.

"Old man, you must have lost your wits to say such things to us!" he cried. "I will never give up Helen. All I can do is to return the treasure – and add my own to it if need be."

Then Priam spoke.

"I agree to everything my son suggests. Let Idaeus go to Agamemnon in the morning, bearing our proposal. If the Achaeans reject it, let him ask them at least to call a brief halt to this accursed war, so we may bury all the dead."

When Idaeus brought the Trojan message to the leaders of the Greeks, Diomedes sprang up and cried:

"Let none of us be duped by Paris' offer – the Trojans are already on the brink of ruin!"

All present shouted their agreement, and turning to the herald Agamemnon said:

"You hear, Idaeus, what answer the Achaeans have given with one voice. As for the dead, however, we have no objection. No one begrudges you the bodies of those who died in battle."

As dawn rose the next day, both Greeks and Trojans hastened to the battlefield and mingled peaceably as each side carried off its corpses. The Achaeans, working through the night as well, also managed to raise the rampart of stones and tree-trunks they had decided on. They built it strong, with tall towers and a protective moat bristling with spikes.

While this was going on, Zeus called all the immortals into his presence and announced:

"Gods and goddesses, pay heed to my orders. From now on, none of you will help either the Achaeans or the Trojans. My word is law – and if any of you flouts it, know that the depths of Tartarus await him, as deep beneath Hades as the heavens are high above the earth. And I can impose my will, for I am far stronger than all of you together. If you wish to test your strength against mine, hang a golden rope down from the skies and try to pull me to the ground, every one of you. I tell you, not one inch will you be able to budge me from high Olympus. But if I wanted to pull you up, I would pull not only you but the whole earth as well. That is how much I surpass you all in might."

The gods bowed their heads in fear; and then Zeus went and sat upon mount Ida, to direct the fighting himself in such a way that the Trojans would prevail and the hour of Achilles' glory come.

With the dawning of the new day the two armies formed opposing ranks once more, ready to do battle. Then Zeus hurled a thunderbolt upon the Danaid hosts who were seized by mindless panic at this evil omen. The Trojans immediately charged and the Achaeans took to their heels with their leaders foremost in the flight. A rout ensued, and woe betide the hindmost. White-haired Nestor found himself in dire distress when an arrow shot by Paris hit one of his horses in the leg. His desperate cries for help went unregarded. Even Odysseus hurried past without pausing to give aid, such terror had Zeus struck in his soul. At last, however, Diomedes espied him, and completely disregarding the great god's wrath he galloped to his side.

"Quick! climb into my chariot!" he cried. "I have Tros' horses, the ones I took from Aeneas; wonderful beasts — they know when to pursue, and when to flee from battle if

needs be. Leave yours to the grooms."

Nestor immediately mounted Diomedes' chariot, seized the reins and cracked the whip. At that moment Hector thundered in to cut off his flight, but Diomedes just had time to cast his spear. Although it missed the Trojan chief it pierced his charioteer, who fell down dead. Hector was heartbroken at the death of his companion, and without a driver he was forced to withdraw from the fighting. Diomedes and Nestor now seized their opportunity and turned upon the Trojans. Such was the fury of their charge they would have sent them fleeing back to Ilium, had Zeus not seen and launched a thunderbolt right at their horses' hooves.

Taken by surprise, Nestor dropped the reins.

"Diomedes," he cried, "Zeus is warning us to leave!"

"I can see that, too," retorted the other, "but I would rather the dark earth opened up and swallowed me than have Hector boast I fled before him to the ships."

Ignoring his protests, the old man turned the chariot and carried them swiftly out of danger, while the son of Priam called out to their backs:

"Diomedes, till now the Achaeans have held you in high honour, but from henceforth they will hold you up to scorn! Run to save yourself, little woman! Hector does not turn to flee! Instead of leaving you to trample Troy and seize our women, he will send you lifeless down to Hades!"

Three times bold Diomedes urged that they turn and face the son of Priam, and three times great Zeus sent his thunderclaps as a sign that victory would be with the Trojans.

Then Hector shouted:

"Hear, o Trojans, Dardanians and Lycians: Zeus is on our side. Advance and cross their moat! Death to the enemy! Spread fire among their ships!"

Then he bent and spoke to his horses.

"Make haste, my steeds. The time has come for you to repay all the care which Andromache lavished on you when she fed you sweet grain and gave you water mixed with wine to drink. Help me now to seize the shield of Nestor and wrench Diomedes' breastplate from his chest. If I can kill these two now, it will be the last night the Achaeans spend on Trojan soil."

Unknown to Zeus, however, Hera was lending secret aid to the Achaeans, who charged into the fight once more with Agamemnon, Menelaus, the two Ajaxes and many others in their front ranks. But the one who wreaked the worst havoc among the Trojans was Teucer, brother of the great Ajax. A deadly archer, he crouched behind his brother's tall shield, and every time Ajax raised it up a moment he would take aim at some figure in the enemy ranks, only waiting to see his victim fall before seeking shelter once again behind the shield, like a child hiding in its mother's skirts.

Seeing the mounting toll, Hector himself galloped up to take on Teucer. Undeterred, the latter shot an arrow at him but killed his charioteer instead. Furious at losing a second driver hard upon the first, the valiant Trojan leapt down from his chariot and, seizing a huge stone, hurled it at Teucer just as he was taking aim at him. It landed on his arm, knocking the bow to the ground. Teucer fell to his knees, clutching his wrist in agony, but Ajax held his shield before him in defence while two faithful comrades dashed in and carried his brother off to safety.

Now Zeus breathed new fire into the Trojans. Led by Hector, they forced the Greek battalions back into the moat again, ruthlessly slaying all stragglers. In their despair, the Achaeans cried out to the heavens for help, but their pleas went unheeded. Finally, each one spurring on his comrades, they managed to form a line before the ships and fought there till night came and battle was abandoned.

"If darkness had not overtaken us," declared Hector, "we would have destroyed the entire Achaean army. However, at first light tomorrow we shall take up arms again to bring destruction on the enemy and joy and glory on ourselves."

While Hector was inspiring his men with these words of hope, in the opposing camp Agamemnon was addressing his generals with a heavy heart.

"These are hard words to utter, yet the bitter truth. Zeus has deceived me, comrades. Although he promised many-towered Troy would fall to me, he now wants me to slink away humiliated, with half my soldiers dead. But if that is how the son of Cronus wants it, we cannot go against his will. Let us board our ships, then, and set sail for our dear homeland."

They all looked at their feet and said nothing, till Diomedes broke the silence with an angry shout:

"You don't know what you're saying, son of Atreus. The Danaids are not afraid to fight. Take your ships and leave, if home is all you think of. I shall stay, with just my men and Sthenelus and fight here till Ilium falls into our hands!"

Diomedes' bold words breathed new fire into them all.

"Son of Tydeus, you are a brave man and have spoken wisely," Nestor told him, "but there is another thing which must be done, and only Agamemnon can do it. I told you before, glorious Atreid, you should not have taken Achilles' prize from him, the fair Briseis; but you ignored me, and in doing so offended the bravest man among us. Listen to me now, and undo the wrong you did to him."

This time, Agamemnon heeded the wise words of white-haired Nestor, and what did he not offer to be reconciled with Achilles! Not only would he give back Briseis — whom he swore to Zeus he had not laid a finger on — but he would offer countless gifts immediately, and many more once they set foot in Troy. Furthermore, when they returned home he would give Achilles one of his daughters in marriage and in addition would hand seven rich cities over to him — and all this if he would but swallow his anger and lead the Achaeans into battle.

This proposal was conveyed to Achilles by Phoenix, Ajax and Odysseus; but the mighty hero's only answer was a withering attack on Agamemnon. And having vented all his bitterness, he concluded with these words:

"I could not bury my wrath, not even if he gave me twenty times more than he possesses, not even all the treasure that passes through Orchomenus or lies in hundred-gated Thebes in Egypt, not even if he gave me as much gold as there is sand on the boundless oceans' shores. No, he and I shall never be reconciled till he has paid more dearly still for the insult he has done me. That is the answer I command you take back to the leaders of the Achaeans. Only leave dear Phoenix with me, he who raised me with his counsels, so that together we may sail for home."

Odysseus and Ajax brought this reply back to Agamemnon, who was sorely troubled when he heard it.

Night was far advanced and all lay down to sleep; but Agamemnon could find no rest. Finally he got up, dressed and went to the doorway of his tent. Opposite, in the Trojan camp, many fires were burning. While he was wondering what this could mean, his brother Menelaus, who could not sleep either, came up and spoke to him.

"Something must be done," they both agreed. "We cannot let our own men sleep untroubled when the Trojans are so close to us." Then, waking all the leaders, they held a war-council.

"We must find out what the Trojans' plans are," Nestor said. "Send two of our men in secretly to see what they can discover."

It was decided that Diomedes and Odysseus should go.

In the opposing camp, Hector, too, was restless. The same thought had occurred to him, and he decided to send a man, Dolon, to spy on the Achaeans. The promise of Achilles' horses as reward was all he needed to persuade him.

Dolon was half-way to the Achaean camp when he blundered into Diomedes and Odysseus. He tried to escape their clutches, but in vain.

"Do not kill me," he begged them on his knees. "My

father will make you rich men if you send me back alive!"

"First tell us why you came and what your side are planning," Odysseus ordered him.

Trembling with fear, Dolon told them everything he knew and more.

"And if you want to wreak real havoc," he added, "go in that direction. There you will find the Thracians, who have just arrived and are sure to be sleeping heavily. Among them is Rhesus, their king, with his splendid horses that are faster than the wind."

By thus betraying the confidence that Hector had placed in him, Dolon imagined he had saved his skin. But who takes pity on a traitor? Diomedes cut him down and without wasting a further moment set off with Odysseus to find the Thracians.

As they expected, every one of them was fast asleep.

"You take the men and I'll go for the horses," Odysseus whispered.

Diomedes fell on them like a lion upon an undefended flock. He killed thirteen, including Rhesus, and would have slain them all had not Athena urged him to leave before the Trojans got wind of his presence.

When Diomedes and Odysseus rode back into camp trailing the horses behind them, everyone gazed in wonder at this prize.

"My old eyes have seen many things," said Nestor, "but never horses such as these."

"They are Rhesus' steeds," Odysseus replied. "Diomedes killed him and twelve of his brave Thracians,

..."You take the men and I'll go for the horses,"
Odysseus whispered...

and before that a spy we met upon our way."

As soon as the sun rose over the horizon, Zeus sent Eris to light the fire of battle once again. The Achaeans were the first to take up arms, and they succeeded in driving the Trojans away from before their ships. But they did not know what the lord of Olympus had in store for them, and so, before the day was out, Agamemnon was wounded in the arm and obliged to withdraw, while Diomedes was hit in the leg pursuing Hector, with an arrow aimed by Paris from afar, and Machaon, the son of Asclepius, was injured as well. This spread consternation among the Achaean host, for he was a skilled surgeon and they had sore need of his services. All these misfortunes were inflicted on them by Zeus, who wished to give victories to the Trojans. Now all fled before the enemy save one, Odysseus. "My soul revolts at the idea of flight," he told himself, "and yet it is a pity to be killed alone." As he stood there undecided, the Trojans ran up and surrounded him. They were running straight into a fire, for Laertes' son fought like a wild beast that a hundred hunting dogs cannot pull down. The first four Trojans who threw themselves upon him suffered instant death. Then he killed the son of Hippasus, brave Charopus, who was fighting at the side of his brother Socus. Seeing his brother's death, Socus cried out like the true hero that he was:

"Renowned Odysseus, first in cunning and in power of mind, today you will either boast that you killed both Hippasus' sons, or you will die beneath my blow." And with these words he flung his spear with all his force at

Odysseus' shield. It pierced the outer layers of leather, tore through the bronze behind, entered his breastplate and cut deep into the skin below the ribs. But Odysseus knew the wound would not prove fatal, and without pulling the spear out from his side he shouted:

"Unhappy youth, if your spear-thrust obliges me to withdraw wounded from the battle, then mine will end your life."

And as the young man turned to save himself, Odysseus' spear caught him in the back. The luckless fellow pitched headlong to the ground, his armour clanging as he fell.

"There's what fate had in store for you, young Socus," said Odysseus, "to give me glory and your soul to Tartarus." And with these words he pulled out Socus' spear which was still buried in his side. Seeing the blood which now gushed out, the Trojans took heart and threw themselves upon him once again. Odysseus then roared out to his comrades to come to his assistance. Three times he shouted and three times Menelaus heard him.

"Odysseus seeks our aid," he said to Ajax. "Come, over here, where the Trojans are thickest on the ground."

They soon made him out, and Ajax immediately dashed to his side. Alarmed by his ferocity and towering stature the Trojans now drew back, whereupon Menelaus grasped Odysseus by the arm and dragged him to the safety of the Achaean lines. While he was doing so, Ajax took furious revenge for the wounding of Odysseus, leaving many of the enemy dead. So murderous was his rage that Hector himself did not dare to face him. Seeing all this from the summit of mount Ida, Zeus put foreboding into Ajax' heart and gave courage to the Trojans. Thus Ajax decided to withdraw, anxious that the Achaean ships might be in danger. Throwing his shield across his back, he turned to run with the Trojans in pursuit. Stopping at intervals to fend them off, he eventually reached the shore.

With the Argive leaders wounded and their men numb with dismay, the Trojans' courage was bolstered further still.

"Brothers," Hector cried, "Zeus is with us! Forward across the moat, and over the ramparts to burn the ships!"

The Trojans heard him and surged forward irresistibly. The Achaeans heard him and drew back in fear. Leaving their chariots by the moat, the Trojans crossed it on foot and reached the ramparts. Some tried to climb them, while others tried to force their way through the gates. A vicious fight developed here, with neither the Trojans able to force their way through, nor the Achaeans to push them back. Standing on the embankment of the moat Hector was urging his soldiers on as they tried to scale the wall when an eagle came into sight high on his left, holding a snake in its talons. Suddenly the snake writhed and sank its fangs into the eagle, which loosed its grip in pain, letting the serpent fall among the Trojans.

On this, the hero Polydamas said to Hector:

"This is a sign from Zeus. Just as that eagle which flew in from our left did not succeed in carrying the snake home to feed its fledglings, so we will fail to scale the wall and burn the ships. It is clear that we must call off our efforts to storm this place. Any soothsayer would tell you the same thing."

"You don't know what you're saying, Polydamas. Why should I place my trust in birds and ignore Zeus' promise to me? I take no heed of portents such as these, whether they be flying to the right, towards the dawn or left, towards the setting sun and darkness. All that has any meaning is to fight with valour for your country!"

With these words the great hero swept into battle like a raging wind, followed by the yelling Trojan throng. Many scaled the rampart and fought there, others dislodged the great stones at its base with crowbars, while others still tried to topple the watch-towers. The Achaeans fought back stubbornly, however. Bitter fighting flared around the tower defended by the Athenians under Menestheus against the attacks of the Lycians led by fearsome Sarpedon and valiant Glaucus. Ajax and Teucer saw the danger and rushed to help Menestheus, but while they were trying to save the Athenians' tower, Zeus led Hector to the main gates.

"Forward, Trojans! the hour has come to breach the Argives' walls!" bellowed the great hero; and seizing a huge boulder, pointed at one end, he hurled it with all his own prodigious strength and as much again lent to him by Zeus, straight into the wooden door of the great gateway. The planks splintered, the hinges tore away and both leaves of the door crashed to the ground. With a fierce look on his face, Hector stormed through the opening, followed by his Trojans, who scaled the wall and began to tear it down, while the Achaeans fled in terror towards their ships.

Satisfied that his aim had been accomplished, Zeus stopped following the battle and turned his eyes peacefully towards the land of the Thracians. Poseidon saw that Zeus' attention was now held by other sights and was so dismayed at the evil turn which the Achaeans' fortunes had taken that he decided to lend them his assistance. He hastened to their camp, and taking on the form of Calchas breathed courage into the two Ajaxes and set them upon Hector. Then he mingled with the warriors who had drawn back and were bewailing the disaster which had overtaken them. Among them were Antilochus, Meriones, Thoas and others. Standing among them, he cried out:

"Shame on you, Argives! You are young and strong and yet you do not fight to save the ships. Who would believe that those same Trojans, who did not dare to venture out beyond their city, would now break down the Danaid gates and storm your ramparts? And all because of Agamemnon's unjust act and Achilles' fearsome wrath. But that does not mean valiant men should lose their heart for battle. I would not waste my time chiding chicken-hearted cowards. No, I am angry with you because you have the spirit and the strength to save the army and yet you do not do so."

Poseidon's words were exactly what was needed. The Achaeans all rose to their feet at once, and seizing their round shields and pointed spears, they ran to join forces with the two Ajaxes. Soon they were fighting with such spirit that, try as desperately as he might, Hector could not move one inch nearer to their ships.

Seeing Poseidon's eagerness to help the Achaeans, Hera devised a cunning means of lulling Zeus' attention longer still.

Having bathed and anointed herself with fragrant perfumes, she adorned herself in all her finery and then tricked Aphrodite into handing over her girdle of love, supposedly so that she might thus reconcile Oceanus and Tethys, who had quarrelled. The truth was that she wanted it for herself and her husband Zeus. Then she persuaded Hypnos, god of sleep, to come with her and help. When the two of them reached mount Ida, Hypnos hid behind a tall fir tree while Hera approached Zeus.

The moment he set eyes on her he was filled with delighted surprise. Seeing her there, so lovely and alluring, he immediately forgot his other cares and desired nothing but her company.

With a look of seeming innocence and a sweet smile on her lips, Hera told him that she was merely passing by on her way to visit Oceanus and Tethys in the hope of bringing them together again.

"You can visit them some other day," purred Zeus. "Stay with me now. I see so little of you, and I've missed you."

Hera's trick had worked. The father of gods and men lay down at her side and soon, with the help of the god Hypnos, whom no power can resist, he fell into a heavy slumber.

His mission accomplished, Hypnos sped to Poseidon.

"Zeus is asleep," he told him, "and will not wake in a

hurry. You are free now to bestow glory on the Achaeans
and wreak destruction on the Trojans."

In an instant, the sea-god changed into a mortal and went
among the Achaeans firing them with zeal. At the same
time, Athena raised Agamemnon and the other wounded
leaders and led them from their tents so that the Greek
hosts might see them at their side and draw courage from
their presence. The two Ajaxes, Teucer, Idomeneus,
Meriones, Menelaus and Antilochus fell like the furies on
the Trojans. In vain did Hector, Aeneas, Paris and Sarpedon try to stem the flood of Achaeans. Great Ajax wrought
fearful havoc in the enemy ranks. Hector bravely ran to
challenge him, and taking careful aim he hurled his spear,
but it landed where the sword and shield straps crossed
upon his chest and so Ajax escaped death. Unshaken by
this narrow shave, he plucked up a boulder as big as a
millstone and set it spinning through the air with horrifying
force, straight into Hector. Like a tall oak struck at the roots
by one of Zeus' fearsome thunderbolts, the valiant son of
Priam toppled senseless to the earth. His spear slipped from
his grasp, his shield dropped and his helmet rolled clatter-
ing on the ground. But Polydamas, Aeneas, Sarpedon and
Glaucus immediately ran up and carried him off before the
Achaeans could seize him.

Hector's injury was a heavy blow to the Trojans, who
now fled for safety before the Danaids' charge.

At this very moment Zeus awoke at Hera's side. As soon
as he had risen he glanced down at the plain below and
could not believe his eyes. The Trojans were fleeing,

...Then he told Iris to go to Poseidon and order him to leave the battlefield at once...

pursued by the Achaeans, and a gasping Hector lay face down on the ground, out of the fight and coughing up dark blood.

Zeus was beside himself with rage, but he knew he owed Hera some explanation for his abrupt change of mood.

"I gave my irrevocable word to Thetis," he explained, "that I would help the Trojans until Achilles had won glory. If any of you immortals dare to assist the Achaeans once again, you will regret it!"

Then he told Iris to go to Poseidon and order him to leave the battlefield at once. Next he called Apollo to him and said:

"Take my shield and brandish it before the Achaeans till they retreat. Then run to Hector and give him new fighting strength to drive the Argive host back to their ships again."

Apollo gladly carried out his orders. When he found Hector, he breathed fresh power into him and commanded him to lead his charioteers once more into the enemy camp. Going on before them, he drove a wide breach through the moat and demolished a section of the wall so that the Trojans could pass through with their horses and chariots.

With Hector at their head, the Trojans poured into Agamemnon's camp. Taken by surprise, the Achaeans scattered in panic, but the brave Aetolian, Thoas, managed to hold some of them together and with Ajax, Idomeneus, Meriones and others they formed a wall bristling with long spears. The Trojans threw themselves upon it but were repulsed with equal violence, and the dead fell thick on both sides without either gaining the advantage. At this moment, Apollo let out a blood-curdling war cry, unbuckled Zeus' shield and lunged forward with it fiercely, scattering the Achaeans in terror, and bringing glory on the Trojans as they cut down the last fleeing stragglers.

"Forward to the ships!" cried Hector. "Leave the dead and the booty. Now is the time to set fire to their vessels."

But on board the ships, Ajax, Teucer and a handful of other bold Achaeans fought back with grim tenacity, plunging their spears into the Trojans as they swept by in their chariots. Through the fearful din of this desperate struggle, Hector spurred his soldiers on:

"Brother Trojans, play the man! Those of you who die in this war are dying for our homeland, dying to save our wives and children and our houses from the flames!"

On the other side, Ajax shouted encouragement to the Achaeans:

"Only if we fight like heroes shall we be saved. If Hector sets fire to the ships then all hope is lost, for the wide sea separates us from our homes. Fight on, for this is a matter of life and death!"

Thus he breathed new fighting spirit into his men and they fought back tooth and nail. But Hector had already reached the ships, and clambering into the bows of one he called out to his men to bring him fire. It was the ship that had brought Protesilaus to Troy, the first Achaean to fall in battle.

Twelve Trojans risked their lives trying to approach that ship; all were dispatched by Ajax, wielding a spear fully twice the normal length. Despite this, the danger to the

Achaean fleet grew steadily more serious.

In Achilles' tent, meanwhile, Patroclus was lamenting the evil fortune which had overtaken the Argive forces.

"Is there no pity in you?" he demanded of the unrelenting hero. "You are no child of Peleus and Thetis. The raging sea and the cruel rocks must have spawned you if you can sit here unmoved while the Achaeans meet their doom. But since you insist on nursing your anger, let me take the Myrmidons and join the fight. All I ask is that you lend me your armour; there's just a chance that the Trojans will mistake me for you and flee in panic." In the end Achilles consented.

"But once you've driven them from the ships," he warned, "don't let success go to your head and chase them all the way to Ilium. Leave them on the plain and come back here. I won't have you risking your neck for Agamemnon, whom I hate more than I have ever hated any man in my whole life."

Meanwhile, Ajax could no longer go on protecting Protesilaus' ship against the will of Zeus. Arrows and spears were whistling all around and bouncing off his shield like rain. Blows fell on him as fast as he could fend them off. His shield arm was numb, his body bathed in sweat and his breath coming in painful gasps, while the Trojans' attacks grew more violent by the moment. Finally Hector swung his sword down on the great spear and sheared off its bronze point. Left with a blunted weapon, the hero could do nothing but withdraw. Resistance was at an end. Then Hector took a burning brand and set fire to the bows of the ship. Little did he know, ill-fated man, that this was all Zeus awaited to cease his aid to the Trojans, and that the smoke which now rose to the heavens from Protesilaus' vessel signalled the beginning of the end of Troy.

Indeed, before the flames could wrap the ship in their embrace, the Myrmidons fell upon the Trojans like a howling storm. Patroclus led the charge in Achilles' gilded chariot, drawn by its splendid and immortal horses with the matchless Automedon at the reins.

When the Trojans saw Patroclus they took him for the fearsome son of Peleus and fled in terror. Stopping only to put out the fire, he took up the pursuit. So relentlessly did he hunt them down that even when they realised that this was not Achilles they continued to withdraw. Now all the Achaeans fought with new determination and cleared the ramparts and the moat of Trojans. The fighting soon moved to the open plain, where Patroclus killed many of the enemy with the help of the other Achaean leaders who were still unwounded.

The Lycian forces suffered particularly badly at Patroclus' hands.

"Shame on you, Lycians," Sarpedon cried out. "Stand your ground. I will march at your head, and then we shall see who this man is who has turned victory into rout!" And with these words he jumped down from his chariot. Patroclus did the same.

Zeus was deeply grieved to see this, for he had fathered Sarpedon and knew it was ordained that his dear son should die in the contest now to come. He even thought of spiriting him away from the battlefield, but was prevented by Hera.

"We other gods do not agree," she told him. "None has the right to change the fate of mortals, not even you. All that remains for you is to ensure that your son is buried with honours in Lycia."

Sarpedon's end was not long coming. Although he charged Patroclus first his spear fell wide. Patroclus did not waste his throw, however; his challenger toppled to the ground like a tall tree beneath the cruel woodsman's axe. Glaucus ran to his side, but it was too late.

"Dear Glaucus," he whispered with his dying breath, "save my body from desecration. Do not let them take my weapons."

Then Glaucus cried out to the Trojan leaders to come and save the hero's body. Polydamas, Aeneas and Hector hastened to the scene, determined to put up a hard fight for the corpse.

But Patroclus had called over Ajax and Teucer, while Meriones and others had also arrived. Bitter fighting now erupted around the dead Sarpedon and Zeus rejoiced to see such toils of war on his dear son's behalf. So many Achaeans and Trojans bit the dust around the hero's body that in the end Zeus decided to let Patroclus have Sarpedon's weapons but to command Sleep and Death to raise the corpse and bear it off to fertile Lycia. Thus the great hero was buried with honours in his homeland and a tall mound raised above him, surmounted by a column.

Once the fighting over Sarpedon was over, Patroclus ordered Automedon to drive the chariot against the Trojan hosts again. In the intoxication of battle he had quite forgotten Achilles' advice and now he began to pursue them right back to the city, inflicting heavy casualties as he advanced. Indeed, he would have taken Troy that day, had not Apollo intervened in her defence. Time and again Patroclus tried to scale the wall, but Apollo always cast him down again, finally crying:

"Retire, brave Patroclus. Troy shall not be taken by your hands, nor even by the hands of Achilles, although he is stronger than you."

At the god's command, Patroclus obeyed and withdrew.

Meanwhile, at the Scaean Gates, Hector stood undecided in his chariot. Should he lead the army into battle or retreat behind the walls? As he was pondering this, Apollo appeared to him in mortal guise and gave him the courage he needed to advance into the fray once more. Patroclus, however, was still fighting like one possessed. Three times he threw himself upon the Trojans, killing nine of them with each attack.

Yet valour alone was not enough, Patroclus; for as you made your fourth charge, your end loomed at your shoulder: Apollo came once more and with his immortal hand he struck you in the back with such a blow that your eyes started from your head. Knocking your helmet to the ground, he snapped your spear in two and wrenched the breastplate from your chest, leaving you a naked and defenceless prey. Then a Dardanian came, the mighty hero Euphorbus, who had killed twenty men so far, and plunged his spear into your body. You did not fall beneath the thrust, however, and he drew out the spear and hid himself among the host, afraid to look you in the face. Then you were struck by Hector's fearsome spear-thrust and you fell like a tall pine with a jarring thud that echoed to the heavens, Patroclus, causing the Achaeans immeasurable grief.

Hector stood over him exulting:

"Ill-starred fool, who thought to plunder Troy and enslave our women! Now you are doomed, and I remain to put the evil day of slavery far from us!"

"Boast all you will, Hector," Patroclus gasped with his dying breath, "yet it was Apollo killed me and not you. Twenty heroes of your kind could not challenge me and live to tell the tale. Do not rejoice too much, for the man still lives who will demand your life in payment for my own."

The moment these words had escaped his lips, thick darkness clouded his eyes. "Do not foretell my downfall," Hector told the dead Patroclus. "How can you know that he of whom you speak will not fall by my hand?" And saying this he hurled himself upon Automedon — but not before Achilles' deathless steeds could gallop him to safety.

The first of the Achaeans to hasten to the defence of Patroclus' dead body was the noble Menelaus. Euphorbus stepped forward menacingly to meet him.

"Get back, Menelaus, or you will meet your death by me. I was the one who struck Patroclus first, and I shall take his weapons."

"You are a valiant spearman, Euphorbus," Menelaus

retorted, "but your brother Hyperenor was a brave man, too
– and I sent him to his death. You sons of Panthous are too
insolent and overbearing. Thus scornfully did Hyperenor
speak to me, down by the ships, brazening it out and saying
that of all the Achaeans I was the most ridiculous. For that
very arrogance he lost his young life to my spear, and now
his good wife weeps for him. Be gone, while you still have
time to regret your rash behaviour."

But Euphorbus held his ground and was the first to
launch his spear; to no avail, however. Menelaus, on the
other hand, hurled his weapon to deadly effect, and the son
of Panthous lost his life and all his war-gear.

As Euphorbus fell, Hector ran up with a strong force of
Trojans. Menelaus looked around and found himself alone.
This forced him to retreat and then Hector grasped his
opportunity and snatched Achilles' splendid weapons from
the dead Patroclus. But Menelaus returned, accompanied
by Ajax. The sight of these two heroes together was too
much for Hector, particularly the towering Ajax, whom he
had always feared.

"You are a coward, Hector," Glaucus shouted, "and not
worthy of your glorious reputation. This is just how the
Achaeans captured Sarpedon's equipment, and they would
have carried off his body, too, if the gods had not borne it
aloft."

"You are a brave man, Glaucus, and the brave do not
speak thus. It is not Ajax that I fear, but Zeus, who can
make the most valiant hero flee. If you think I lack the
courage to fight for Patroclus' body, just stand by me and

see." And with these words he turned to the Trojans.

"Advance, my heroes! Stop them from taking Patroclus, while I put on Achilles' armour."

Hector quickly donned the son of Peleus' shining breastplate, snatched up his shield and ran to join the fighting.

It broke Menelaus' heart to see his enemy wearing the trappings which the gods had once presented to Peleus, which he in turn had passed on to Achilles and which Achilles had then lent to Patroclus for the good of all the Argives. Yet here they were now, gleaming on Hector's body and in his hands. However, his thoughts quickly turned again to the dead Patroclus, and he shouted out to the Achaean leaders with every ounce of strength left in his

lungs, for the Trojans were milling all around him and he had only Ajax at his side.

"Heroic Danaids!" he cried, "Woe betide us if we leave Patroclus to become food for the Trojan hounds!"

Many heard him and ran to reach there first. None, however, could outstrip the other Ajax, son of Oileus. Seeing their enemies approach, the Trojans made haste to drag away the body, but the two Ajaxes charged in and forced them to retire. The Trojans made a second sally and Hector flung his spear at the Great Ajax. It missed him by a hairsbreadth, but struck down Schedius, the bravest of the Phocians. Ajax killed the hero Phorcys in reprisal and at this the Trojans retreated once again in terror, Hector with them. Now the Achaeans would have set off in pursuit, had

not Apollo thrown Aeneas into the fight, who gave the
Trojans new heart by killing one of the enemy. Again the
fighting flared up around Patroclus' body, the advantage
now with one side, now the other, but neither willing to
give up the struggle. The Achaeans told themselves: 'Better
the earth should open up and swallow us than leave Patroclus to the enemy, to be dragged inside their walls and put
to shame.' As for the Trojans, they said to one another:
'Even if it is written that we shall all be killed, to die close
to this man makes it all worthwhile!'

A little further off, Achilles' steeds, knowing who had
been slain, whinnied their grief; and for all Automedon's
sweet words of comfort to them they stood numbly between the shafts of their magnificent chariot, their heads
drooping to the ground and their warm tears watering the
earth while the battle raged unquenchable beyond them.

Finally Ajax decided that Achilles must be warned; and
since Menelaus could not bear to leave Patroclus' corpse
for long, he ran to find Antilochus, son of Nestor. Surprised
and saddened, for he had not yet heard that Patroclus was
dead, Antilochus took the sad news to the son of Thetis.

Returning immediately to the battlefield, Menelaus said
to Ajax:

"Achilles will not come, I fear; he does not have his
weapons. We must see how we can best escape death and
recover the body unaided."

"You are right. The best thing would be for you and
Meriones to run and lift the body up just as we others
launch an attack upon the Trojans."

This diversion gave Menelaus and Meriones time to hoist Patroclus on their shoulders. Surrounded by their comrades, they withdrew towards the ships. Seeing the body being carried off, the Trojans charged in furious pursuit. The two Ajaxes turned to check them, and yet again the fighting flared. Hector and Aeneas fought their way so close that at one moment it seemed that the struggle for Patroclus would have no end.

Eventually Achilles saw his compatriots in the distance, returning in disorder. Fear sprang into his mind, fear of the evil fortune that had indeed befallen his dear friend.

"He did not listen to me," he groaned. "Brave Patroclus has been killed." Yet he wanted to be sure.

At that very moment the son of renowned Nestor arrived, bearing the ill tidings. Grief wrapped Achilles like a heavy shroud. His mourning was terrible to behold. Filling his hands with ashes, he scattered them upon his head and smeared his handsome face. Then he flung himself into the dust, twisting and tearing out his hair. Suddenly he let out a terrifying groan that echoed over the horizon, losing itself in whispers on the broad reaches of the sea. His mother Thetis heard him and rose up from the waters. In tears, she asked what fresh great evil had befallen him.

"My friend Patroclus has been killed, mother, he whom I honoured above all my comrades. I have lost him, and together with him all my weapons. The murderer Hector has them in his grasp, miracle weapons, the like of which the world has never seen. I have brought you nothing but sorrow, mother — and the greatest grief of all is soon to come, for I know my days are numbered; but first Hector must be toppled in the dust. As for the rest, it matters but little to me now."

Knowing the black fate written for her son, Thetis could do nothing to restrain him; but she did promise to bring him, at first light, a new set of shining armour forged by the immortal Hephaestus.

While she departed immediately for Olympus to beg fresh weapons of the famous craftsman, the Achaeans were still putting up a despairing struggle to keep the dead Patroclus out of the pursuing Trojans' clutches, for Hector and Aeneas fought on with fiery and unflagging zeal. Three times the son of Priam caught Patroclus by the feet and three times the two Ajaxes forced him to let go his hold. But like a hungry lion that sees its prey being snatched away, he would have seized Patroclus in the end, had Hera not warned Achilles to go just as he was and stand above the moat in full view of the Trojans, in the hope that this might take the wind out of their sails and give the Achaeans a breathing-space.

The hero heeded the goddess' advice, and standing on the earthen bank that rimmed the moat he let out a blood-curdling war cry. Athena gave a deafening shout as well and their combined voices sowed blind panic in the Trojan ranks. Their horses turned and galloped off unchecked, and wild confusion reigned. But what terrified them most of all was the unearthly glow which appeared above Achilles' head. At the sight of this, twelve brave Trojans fell dead in sheer terror, and the Achaeans were able to carry Patroclus

..."My friend Patroclus has been killed, mother, he
whom I honoured above all my comrades."...

away to a safe distance and place him on a funeral bed.

Achilles received his lifeless friend in silent grief, but his tears revealed the unbearable pain he felt.

At the request of Hera, the sun-god Helius made haste to hide his fiery disc beneath the horizon and thus the third and dreadful day of fighting drew swiftly to its close, a day that had opened, just as Zeus had willed it, with the wounding of Agamemnon and the other Achaean leaders and had ended with the death of Patroclus and the bitter struggle to save his body from defilement.

This night, too, the Trojan leaders met in council. The reappearance of Achilles had filled them with foreboding. Polydamas urged that they take advantage of the darkness to barricade themselves behind the city-walls once more. Hector, however, would not agree to this.

"We must give battle where the ships are drawn up, exactly where Zeus led us," he maintained, "and if Achilles comes out once more, I shall not flee but stand to face him – and may the best man win. I still believe that Ares is just and will punish the aggressor."

Fair words these may have been, but far from wise; yet the Trojans were persuaded, for Athena had taken away their power of judgement and thus none of them was willing to heed Polydamas' prudent counsels.

Meanwhile, Hephaestus had laboured at his forge all night to make new armour for Achilles. The blacksmith of the gods had never forgotten Thetis' help when she found him abandoned on the isle of Lemnos, and now he worked with eager zeal to please her. "When mortal eyes behold these, they'll be dazzled," he told her as he set to work.

Before day dawned, Hephaestus' task was finished. The gold and silver-decorated weapons gleamed and sparkled in the sun. The rich adornment and the human figures which the god had sculpted on the great round shield were a delight for the eye to behold. The gods themselves would have been dazzled by the beauty of those arms, let alone mere mortals.

Early in the morning, Thetis brought the gleaming armour to Achilles. She found him holding Patroclus in his arms and weeping; but the moment he set eyes on her he felt a surge of savage joy. the hour of his revenge was drawing near.

"Arm yourself now," his mother told him, "but first call all the Achaeans together in council; and speaking gently, with restraint, cleanse your soul of its wrath against Agamemnon. The body I will take care of myself, dripping ambrosia and nectar on it, so it remains unspoiled."

Achilles followed his mother's advice. Leaving his tent, he roused the host, calling them to council. They all came running, even those who never ventured out beyond the ships, such as the cooks and the storemen. Not one remained behind, for the Achilles whom all of them loved so dearly was back with them once more. Limping badly and leaning on their sticks came Diomedes and Odysseus, whose wounds still gave them pain. Last to arrive was Agamemnon, his wounded arm wrapped up in bandages. When they were all assembled, the son of Peleus rose to his feet and said:

"Son of Atreus, would that that which came between us had never happened. Only the Trojans have profited by it. As for the Achaeans, they shall remember our quarrel for all time. Only one thing matters now, however: to take the fight to the enemy, united once again."

When they heard Achilles speak these words, they were filled with a joy beyond belief.

"I have often been taken to task for the evil which I did you," Agamemnon confessed. "It did not happen of my own free will. Almighty Zeus had deprived me of my wits, and cursed Ate, goddess of ill-fortune, blinded me. Who is proof against the power of Ate? Not even all-powerful Zeus himself. But now, son of Peleus, I shall give you all I promised yesterday through Odysseus. Let the younger ones go to bring them now, although I know you are in haste to fight."

Nestor's sons ran and brought the gifts from the tent of the great Atreid, with first and foremost the lovely Briseis, accompanied by seven of the choicest hand-maids, these, too, a gift from Agamemnon to Achilles.

As soon as Briseis saw Patroclus lying dead, she fell upon his body with sobs which seemed torn from the very depths of her soul.

"I left you living and now I find you dead. Oh, Patroclus, sweet-voiced Patroclus, who would not leave me weeping but comforted me when misfortune and death were visited upon my family. You told me you would make me Achilles' wife and that our wedding-table would be richly spread, in Phthia, among the Myrmidons."

The tears streamed down her cheeks as she sobbed out these words, and at her side the other women mourned, remembering their own heartaches and disappointments.

Soon the fighting would begin. The whole army sat down first to eat but Achilles could not touch a thing. Fortunately Athena noticed this and dripped ambrosia and nectar into his veins so that hunger would not sap his strength. The two armies quickly buckled on their weapons and were soon in a state of readiness. Achilles mounted his chariot, shining like the sun in his brilliantly-polished armour. Beside him, Automedon took up the reins, waiting for his order to whip the horses into a gallop.

Zeus was watching everything from the heavens, and told the gods that they were now free to help whichever side they wished. He hoped for an evenly-matched strug-gle, lest Achilles in his burning fury take Troy that very day and thus erase what Destiny had written.

The battle started. As long as the gods still kept their distance, the Achaeans triumphed under Achilles and the Trojans were in continual retreat; but when the immortals threw themselves into the fighting, it became a terrifying clash of equals. On one side Zeus hurled down his thunder-bolts, while on the other Poseidon shook the earth. Mount Ida, Troy, the Achaean ships and all creation shuddered with such violence that Hades feared the earth might split and bathe the dark kingdom of the underworld in light. In all this deafening chaos Achilles searched for Hector; but instead Aeneas stepped up to challenge him.

"What sends you seeking battle with me?" Achilles

asked ironically. "Do you imagine, Aeneas, that if you killed me old Priam would hand his kingdom over to you when he already has so many children waiting for the throne? Besides, have you forgotten how I hunted you across the slopes of Ida? So get out while you can, before they say, when it's too late, what a rash fool you were to provoke the great Achilles."

"Don't think you frighten me, son of Peleus. I can be insulting too. But what's the point, when each of us knows so many oaths that a galley with a hundred oars would sink beneath their weight? Men's tongues can say a lot, but what comes of it? You get as good as you give! So let's not squabble like two housewives in the middle of the street. It's time for our spears to speak instead; and let Zeus decide which of us will suffer death and which win glory."

The duel began. They fought first with their spears, next with swords and then even with stones. Aeneas put up a heroic and skilled struggle but his opponent was far superior to him. For all this, Aphrodite's son refused to withdraw.

Poseidon now began to get uneasy, even though he had no affection for the Trojans. 'Achilles will kill him,' he told himself, 'and then Zeus will be furious, for the Fates have written that Aeneas the Dardanian will become ruler of whatever Trojans escape the final slaughter.'

And with these words he cast a cloud before Achilles' eyes, then took Aeneas up and carried him off far to the rear and out of danger.

The son of Thetis realised what had happened and said:

...Poseidon cast a cloud before Achilles' eyes, then
took Aeneas up and carried him off...

"The gods love Aeneas. Men are right when they say he is the son of Aphrodite."

This said, he urged the Achaeans on against the Trojans. Hector did likewise and a full-scale battle was soon in progress. However, Apollo made sure that Hector could not approach Achilles, who soon succeeded in splitting the Trojan forces in two. Half were now fighting the Achaeans on the plain, while the remainder he forced back upon the Scamander, the sacred river which the immortals called the Xanthus. A bloody conflict developed on its banks, two sons of Priam, Lycaon and Polydorus, soon falling prey to Achilles' deadly spear. Blood was the only balm for the savage anger which had possessed the son of Peleus since the death of his dear friend. His heart had turned to iron and there was no salvation for those who fell into his clutches. Thus, although he captured twelve Trojan warriors and did not kill them outright, it was not out of pity but implacable desire for revenge: he was keeping them to sacrifice at Patroclus' burial as a final tribute to his dead companion.

The battle on the bank of the Scamander raged on un-abated. The Myrmidons tore the Trojan troops to shreds. Never till now had Achilles killed so many of them. The Xanthus' waters ran dull red with blood and its bed filled with the lifeless corpses of the enemy, until the river-god, unable to stomach any more, sent a wall of raging flood-spate down to engulf the Myrmidons and Achilles with them. The mighty hero would have drowned ingloriously had Hera not sent warning to Hephaestus, who sped to tame the river by drying its course up with his searing fire.

Saved by Hephaestus' unexpected aid, Achilles fell with fresh wrath on the Trojans, who now fled for refuge behind the tall walls of their city. Watching the rout from high on the ramparts, Priam ordered the great gates to be opened wide and let the army through. Exhausted, with parched throats and white with dust, the Trojans retired from the plain, pursued relentlessly by Achilles, whose spear wrought havoc in their ranks. In such swathes did he cut them down, he would have swept into the city irresistible, had Apollo not employed a trick against him and inspired a brave and noble youth, Agenor, son of wise Antenor, with the courage and faith to believe that he could slay Achilles and save Troy.

Filled with determination, young Agenor stood his ground against the rampaging son of Peleus and hurled his spear. It struck him in the leg, but Hephaestus' well-wrought armour did its work and the weapon glanced aside. Then Achilles flung his deadly lance, and he aimed well; but the alert Apollo darted in at the last moment and lifted up Agenor, concealing him within a cloud. Then the god took on the form of the young hero and began to run, drawing Achilles far off from the gates. By the time the god resumed his divine aspect it was too late for the furious Achilles to do anything: the Trojans were all safely within the city.

But there was one who had not sought the safety of the walls and stood alone before the Scaean Gates. This was Hector, whose harsh fate bound him there to await a fearsome enemy thirsting for revenge. High above him on the ramparts, Priam and Hecabe begged him tearfully to retreat into the city, but Hector was deaf to their entreaties, and in the meantime Achilles was approaching fast.

Priam was the first to make him out, glinting in his polished armour like Sirius, the bright star that comes above the horizon in the autumn and brings nothing but ill-fortune to mankind.

"If the gods desired his downfall as I do," Priam muttered, "the jackals and the vultures would pick his bones clean in an instant, and the crushing weight of grief for all my brave sons he has slaughtered would be lifted from my shoulders."

But the gods had other plans, and Achilles came bounding closer, snarling like a starving lion that leaps to tear its prey to shreds, while the unhappy Hector stood rooted to the spot as the choices facing him flashed through his mind.

"If I run for the cover of the walls, Polydamas will immediately reproach me that he advised retreat into the city long ago. I did not heed his warning and brought destruction on our army. Now there is only one course open to me: to stand and face Achilles, and either kill him and save Troy or die before this sacred city."

Yet when he saw the son of Peleus charging down upon him, his armour blazing like a flaming fire, Hector, for all his valour, suddenly lost heart and could not stand to face his foe. And so, leaving the gates behind him, he began to run beneath the walls. Confident in the swiftness of his feet, Achilles took off after him. Sprinting with equal swiftness, Hector first passed the watch-tower where the windswept

fig tree grew, then struck out on the carriage road, with his
enemy in pursuit, until he reached the fountains where two
springs of the Scamander gushed out, one hot and one cold.
How lovely this spot was in peaceful times, when the
Trojan women and their lovely daughters washed their
well-woven robes in its broad stone basins! Now it was
witness to a brave man fleeing one even braver. The prize
in this race, though, would not be a roast ox or the pelt of
some prized animal, but the life of noble Hector. And as a
fawn cannot escape a hunting-dog, so he could not outrun
fleet-footed Achilles. However many times he tried to
reach the towers which flanked the Dardanian Gates, the
other would head him off and force him out towards the
plain. Just as in a dream, when you cannot shake your
pursuer off nor he lay hands on you, so it was here; however much speed Apollo lent to Hector's feet, he could not
draw away. And as they ran Achilles gestured to his army
not to try shooting Hector with their bows, lest some archer
find his mark and win the glory for himself. Three times
they raced around the walls of Troy, but when they reached
the springs again Zeus lifted his golden scales and placed a
fate upon each pan, Achilles' on the one and Hector's on
the other. The scales tipped down heavily on Hector's side,
pointing the way to Hades. Then Apollo left his side, and
blue-eyed Athena ran to halt this endless race.

"Stop and take a breath, Achilles," she said to him. "The
hour has come for us to kill brave Hector and win great
glory for ourselves."

And having said this to the one, she went to the other

and created the illusion that his brother Deiphobus was standing at his side, thus giving Hector the courage that he needed to stand up to Achilles.

"I will flee from you no more, son of Peleus," he cried. "My soul exhorts me to do battle with you. The time has come to kill you or be killed. But let us swear a solemn oath before the gods. If I kill you, I shall take your weapons and your armour, but your body I shall render to the Achaeans. You will do the same for me, if I fall at your hands."

Achilles returned his fair words with an angry glare.

"Hector, I have not forgotten what you did," he growled, "so do not talk to me of terms. Just as lions and men can swear no oaths between them, and the wolf does not discuss conditions with the lamb, neither can we two agree and exchange promises. Now the hour has come for one of us to sate Hades with his blood – so just remember all your skill in war, and fight like the good and valiant spearman that you are. Yet there is no escape for you, since I have Athena on my side. The time has come for you to pay for all my comrades that you slaughtered when you ran berserk with your long spear."

Then, without a word of warning, he hurled his fearsome lance; but noble Hector quickly ducked, and passing overhead it buried itself in the ground. Athena plucked it out and returned it to Achilles while Hector, who had noticed nothing, was saying:

"You see, you missed me, son of Peleus, for all your boasts that you had one of the immortals on your side. You

...Achilles attacked simultaneously, his heart brimming over with fierce hatred...

thought your threats would make me lose my courage, but
do not wait for me to turn and flee so you can drive your
sword into my back. No, strike me in the chest as I charge
down on you – but first you'll have to escape my own spear
if you can. Ah, may it run you through! If you were spitted
the fight would be much easier for the Trojans, for you're
the greatest curse to all of us!"

With this, he hurled the long shaft with terrifying force,
right at the centre of Achilles' shield. But how was it to
pierce the handiwork of a god? Sadly Hector watched it
rebound and glance off far away – and he had no other
spear.

"Deiphobus!" he shouted then, "Give me your spear,
quickly!" In vain he called out to the empty air, for his
brother was far away in fortress Troy. "Athena has tricked
me," Hector muttered. "There is no one at my side but
death; but I shall go down fighting!" Without hesitating for
a moment he drew out his keen sword and, bending low,
began to charge with ever-increasing speed, his blade held
out before him, like some eagle swooping from the clouds
on a defenceless lamb. Achilles attacked simultaneously,
his heart brimming over with fierce hatred. Just as the
Evening Star shines bright in the night sky, so gleamed the
well-honed blade at the tip of his lance, as he drew it back
in his right hand to hasten Hector's downfall. He looked at
him and hatred rose like bile. His enemy was cased from
head to foot in his own armour, which he had taken from
Patroclus' corpse, but a small area of Hector's neck was
left exposed, just the spot where death can enter quickly.

And as Hector threw himself in desperation on his foe, Achilles coolly jabbed at him with his long spear, exactly in the spot he'd aimed for, so he would not lose the power of speech before he died. Hector tumbled in the dust, and standing over him Achilles cried out boastfully:

"So, Hector, you thought you'd go unpunished when you stripped Patroclus of my arms. It did not cross your mind, you fool, that there was one left braver still to exact vengeance for his death. Now you will be devoured by dogs and buzzards, while the Achaeans will deck him out in all the splendour he deserves."

"I implore you, by all you hold most sacred," whispered Hector with his dying breath, "do not leave me carrion for your hounds. My father will give you all the gold and copper you desire if you but give my body to be buried by the Trojans and their women."

"Spare your breath, jackal," was Achilles' cruel retort. "The harm that you have done me is so great that I wish I could devour your raw flesh. Nothing in this world could make me feel the slightest pity for you. Were they to bring me twenty times more ransom and promise me as much again; nay, were Priam to offer me your weight in gold I would not give up your corpse for your mother to weep over but will throw you to the camp dogs and the birds of prey, to tear you into pieces."

As his spirit left him, Hector groaned:

"I knew that you were not to be persuaded, for your heart is cold and hard as iron. Only consider how much you will anger the gods by this, because your own end is approaching, too."

The shadow of death fell over him as he gasped these words, but Achilles went on speaking to the corpse:

"You go on down to Hades, and I'll accept my death if that is what Zeus and the other gods have in store for me."

With this parting shot he began to strip the body, re-claiming his armour and his splendid weapons. The other Achaeans crowded round to admire the dead man's splendid build and handsome face; and not one of them left without inflicting some further wound on him. "How much softer Hector has grown now," someone jeeringly re-marked, "than when he burned our ships with his dread fire!"

As this was going on, Achilles' thoughts turned to Pa-troclus, lying unwept and unburied at the ships, and a sudden, hideous inspiration came to him. Piercing the flesh above dead Hector's heels, he passed through leather thongs and tied them to his chariot. Then he jumped on board, carrying the famous armour with him and brought his whip down on the horses' backs. They willingly leapt forward, dragging the ill-starred Hector off in clouds of dust. His hair was thrown into disorder and his once-handsome face besmirched with earth — the earth of his own native land; but Zeus himself had decreed this would be so.

Up on the ramparts, his mother tore her hair out at the roots and his father Priam moaned like an animal in pain. All wept at the sight, and mourning swept like fire from one end of the city to the other.

Inside the palace, Andromache sat weaving at her loom in blissful ignorance, for no messenger dared to go and tell her that Hector had been left outside the gates. But when she heard the wails of sorrow she went out in the street and began to run towards the ramparts like a thing possessed. From on high she saw the appalling sight: Hector being cruelly dragged by the swift horses towards the Achaean ships. She could not endure it long. Dark night rushed into her eyes and she fell down in a faint. When she came round she burst into a fit of sobbing. She thought how much her own black fate resembled that of Hector. Then her thoughts turned to her baby son Astyanax; even if he should escape the sword, he would grow up neglected and despised, like every orphan.

"Ah, Hector," she moaned, "was this what fate decreed for you: to be dragged from our sides and devoured by the hounds of the heartless Achaeans?"

While the Trojans mourned for Hector, the Achaeans had reached the ships and each gone off to his own vessel; but Achilles did not dismiss the Myrmidons.

"Let us stand here in full armour by our horses and weep for Patroclus," he said. "The mourning of his friends is the greatest honour a dead man can have. When we have no more tears to shed, we shall set the horses loose and sit to eat here all together."

With these words he let out a loud cry of grief and began the dirge. The Myrmidons followed suit immediately, and led their horses three times round the body. Thetis herself, invisible, watered the well-springs of their tears, and so violent was their weeping that it soaked their armour and the sand beneath their feet.

"Let your soul rejoice now, Patroclus!" cried Achilles. "It was for you that I dragged Hector here, for you that I shall sacrifice twelve brave Trojan warriors on your funeral pyre!" And pulling Hector by the hair, he flung him face-down in the dust next to Patroclus' bier.

When all had sobbed until their eyes were dry, he made them sit down by the ship and served the traditional rich meal of consolation.

That night, exhausted by his pursuit of Hector, Achilles lay down on the sand and was overcome by sleep. Then, in a dream, he saw Patroclus standing over him, begging that the funeral take place without delay so that his spirit might be set free by the flames.

"When you have burned me," he added, "place my bones in the same urn which will later hold your own. Since the day your father took me into his house, nothing has ever separated us. Let it be so in death, as well."

Deeply moved, Achilles stretched his arms out to Patroclus, but they embraced empty air. He woke with his friend's words engraved upon his soul. Everything would be done as he had requested.

At the first light of dawn the Myrmidons began to bring in wood on pack animals. When a huge quantity had been gathered they stacked it up into a towering funeral pyre. In solemn mourning they placed Patroclus on its summit. Achilles cut off and offered him locks of his hair. He had been saving them for the river-god Sperchius, but now he knew he was destined never to return to Phthia he gave them to his friend. Then many animals were sacrificed, to be consumed in the flames along with the dead man; and finally Achilles with his own hand slew and offered to Patroclus the twelve valiant Trojans which some evil instinct had driven him to capture by the Scamander for just this purpose.

"Let your soul rejoice, Patroclus," he cried out, "yes, even in the dark place it now wanders in — for I have carried all out as I promised you. But the liberating fire shall not have Hector's body. The hounds alone will have that."

Yet the gods would not allow the Trojan hero's corpse to be treated with such scorn. Night and day Aphrodite kept the dogs at bay and anointed the dead body with oil of roses to prevent it being torn and bruised. And Apollo hid the sun behind black clouds so its harsh rays would not parch the flesh and rob dead Hector of his beauty.

Patroclus' funeral pyre was set ablaze with the aid of Boreas and Zephyrus, gods of the wind. Achilles paced round it tirelessly the whole night through, pouring libations of wine upon the earth for the rest of his friend's soul, and rending the heavens with his cries of grief. Only when the Morning Star rose up over the horizon and the fire died down to embers did he stretch himself exhausted on the ground for a short while and let sleep overtake him. Yet not for long — for when dawn broke and the whole host of the Achaeans gathered round the smouldering ashes, he rose and went up to Agamemnon and the other leaders.

"Son of Atreus and all you rulers of the Achaean league," he said, "first douse the fire well with wine, then gather up Patroclus' bones. You will know them from the others because they lie in the pyre's heart. Place them in a golden urn until the time comes for my own to join them there. Then raise a tomb as lofty as befits him. Later, when you lay me in there too, build the tomb wider and still taller."

All was done as Achilles had commanded, but he would not let the Achaeans depart. He wished to honour Patroclus with funeral games. Giving orders for a stadium to be laid out, he brought up various prizes from the ships: cauldrons, tripods, horses, mules and oxen, lovely slave-girls and grey iron ingots, which all who took part in the games would share, the richest prizes going to the winners. The army's most renowned heroes distinguished themselves in the events: chariot-racing, boxing, wrestling, running, hand-to-hand combat, discus, archery and spear-fighting.

With these games, the funeral ceremonies came to an end and the period of deep mourning was over. But not for all, for Achilles could not put Patroclus from his mind and grieved unceasingly for his valiant and impetuous friend. He would throw himself face down upon the ground or lie despairingly staring at the sky, then suddenly leap to his feet as if confused and make off for the seashore. Sometimes he would harness his horses to the chariot, tie Hector by the feet behind and drag him round Patroclus' grave. Twelve days Achilles maltreated Hector's body in this way, until Zeus called for Thetis and told her to go and ask her

son to accept a ransom and give old Priam back his dead
son's remains, if he did not wish to incur the wrath of the
lord of gods and men. Then he sent Iris to Priam to tell him
he could enter Achilles' tent unharmed and ask for Hector's
corpse in return for splendid gifts.

Achilles reluctantly submitted to Zeus' will but Priam
listened with relief, having already decided he would go
down on bended knee and beg his son back, come what
may. Straightway he ordered his other sons to prepare his
chariot and a sturdy four-wheeled waggon drawn by mules.
Then he called Hecabe and told her what he had decided.

"You must be mad to think of doing such a thing," she
cried. "The savage will tear you limb from limb!"

Ignoring her protests, Priam took Hecabe by the hand
and together they went to open the locked chamber where
all their most precious possessions were kept safely in
carved wooden chests From them he took twelve splendid
blankets, twelve rugs, as many snow-white cloaks and then
an equal number of fine robes. Next he weighed out ten
talents of gold and added two gleaming tripods, four
cauldrons and finally a precious cup, a gift of priceless
value from the Thracians. Not even this did he begrudge, so
desperately did he wish to hold his dead son in his arms
again! Then he left the room, but in his haste it seemed to
him that all the Trojans in the palace courtyard were delib-
erately trying to block his passage.

"Out of my way, you miserable idlers!" he cried out
testily. "What are you doing here? Have you no dead of
your own to mourn and come to make my grief more bitter

still? Now he is gone, you cowards, you shall learn all too soon how great is the disaster which has fallen on us all. Ah, could I but go down to Hades first, rather than see our city delivered to the flames!"

As he elbowed a passage through the crowd, he broke out in recrimination against his sons, Helenus, Paris, Deiphobus and the others, who had not yet come in answer to his call.

"Make haste, you spineless scum! Show your sheepish faces! Would you had all been killed instead of Hector. I had so many valiant sons, but all of them are fallen in battle. Only the useless dregs are left, the liars and cheats who steal the meat out of my people's mouths. Run and prepare the chariots I asked you for, and carry the gifts we took out of the chests. I am impatient to pay Hector's ransom!"

Cowed by their father's lashing tongue, they ran to carry out his orders. Then Priam called his faithful herald Idaeus to his side, a man advanced in years like his master. He instructed him to drive the waggon, in which they placed the treasure, while he himself would take the chariot reins.

They went down through the city, a weeping crowd accompanying them until they reached the Scaean Gates. Darkness was well advanced before they reached the tomb of Ilus and stopped to let the horses drink.

Suddenly they saw a smooth-cheeked youth approaching. He looked like some young princeling but in fact he was Hermes, sent that way by Zeus.

"Where are you going in the dead of night, old man, and

carrying such a precious cargo?" Hermes asked. "Do you not fear the Achaeans? Tell me where you are headed and let me guide you there, for you remind me of my dear father. Do not be afraid of me, even though I am a Myrmidon and a companion of the man who killed your son."

"If you are in Achilles' company, then tell me, I beg you, does my son's body still exist, or has it been devoured by the hounds?"

"Neither the dogs have eaten it nor the vultures. It lies unharmed, close to Achilles' ship. However ruthlessly he drags it in the dust he cannot spoil its beauty. This is the twelfth night now, and yet the corpse is cool and fresh. The blood that smeared it has been washed away and all the wounds have closed, even those inflicted after death. Your son was beloved of the gods, old man."

The delighted Priam made as if to offer a fine chalice to the noble youth, saying, "Just help me to reach Achilles' tent."

"I cannot accept a gift, lest I incur his wrath," the other replied, "but I will willingly accompany you as far as renowned Argos, if need be." And with these words Hermes led Priam to Achilles, without a single Myrmidon observing them. To enter the courtyard where the tent was pitched, they had to open a gate held closed by a bolt so heavy that it took three men to draw it back. Only Achilles could open it unaided; yet Hermes slid it out without the slightest difficulty, and they entered without the wheels or horses' hooves making the faintest sound.

"We are here, old man," their guide announced, "and

now I must leave you. Know that I am Hermes, and was sent by Zeus to help you. Enter the tent now and make your plea to him in the fairest words you know."

Priam climbed down from the chariot, leaving Idaeus to hold the horses, and went into the tent alone. Achilles was sitting at the table with Automedon and Alcimus and there were others in the background. Priam went down before Achilles, grasped his knees and kissed his hands, those terrible hands that had slain so many of his sons.

Achilles was taken aback to find the saintly Priam at his feet. The others in the tent looked at one another in dumb astonishment.

"Think of your own father, illustrious Achilles," he entreated. "Who knows what agonies he endures on your

behalf? Yet at least he knows you live and hopes to see you once again. I, though, am the most tragic father of them all. Fifty sons I had, but the greatest number, and the bravest, have been slain by you and your Achaean comrades. And he who was his city's only shield you killed a few days past as he struggled to defend his homeland. It is to plead for him that I have come to the Achaean ships tonight, bringing a generous ransom with me. Respect the gods, Achilles, remember your own father, and take pity on him who has brought himself to do that which no other mortal upon earth could bear: to kiss the hands of the man who killed so many of his sons."

Achilles wept to hear the old man's words, and all wept with him. Priam wept too, for his dead boy. Gently the son of Peleus prised the unhappy father's hands from round his knees. Then, rising to his feet, he lifted him, took his arm and said:

"Unhappy, grey-haired man, it is true that you have suffered many griefs. What love and courage could have brought you to the Achaeans' ships, to face the man who has done you such great evil? But come, sit down. Nothing can come of bitter mourning. My father, too, is an unhappy man, for all that the gods loved him. They gave him a goddess for a wife, then granted him only brief joy and long sadness. I am his only son, and yet he lost me when I had hardly grown to manhood because I came here to bring ruin upon your sons and you. But his cruellest grief of all is that he knows my life has but a brief span yet to run and he will never see his son again. Like my father, you were happy once, surpassing all the kings who bordered you in wealth and royal sons; but all the gods have brought you in the end is ruin and deep sorrow. Yet bear your burden patiently, for nothing will come of weeping. Here, sit down for a moment."

"Do not ask me to be seated as long as Hector lies out there untended. Accept the ransom and give me leave to see him — and may the gods grant you a safe journey home, since you have spared my life."

"Do not press me, old man. I will give you Hector. How could I say no, when Zeus himself desires it! Besides, do you think I do not understand that some immortal led you here? No ordinary man could have got past the guards or drawn the bolt of the courtyard gate unaided."

Then he went out with Automedon and Alcimus, un-
hitched the horses, took the ransom off the waggon and
invited Idaeus to come and sit inside the tent. But of the
gifts they left behind two long cloaks and a robe to wrap
the dead man in. Then Achilles ordered his slave-girls to
bathe Hector's body, fearing that if he saw it streaked with
earth Priam would lose his self-control and drive Achilles
to kill the old man in rekindled anger, thus scorning Zeus'
will.

When Hector had been washed, Achilles wrapped the
body in the robes himself, then laid it on a couch which he
placed in the long waggon. The moment he had done so he
burst into tears.

"Do not be angry with me, Patroclus, for giving Hector
back. It was the gods that willed it so. And of the precious
ransom paid for him I shall single out the choicest items for
you."

Then he went inside the tent again and said to Priam:

"Your son has been freed. He is lying in the waggon,
covered with a cloak. You can see him when you take him
away at daybreak. Meanwhile, sit down, for it is time to
eat."

Over dinner, he asked Priam:

"Now, old man, how many days' truce do you need from
the fighting to carry out the burial? Tell me, and I shall
personally hold the army back."

"You would be a generous foe to give me all I ask – nine
days, say, to mourn him, a tenth to burn his pyre and eat the
funeral baked meats, and the eleventh to raise his burial

mound. On the twelfth day let us fight again, if it must be so."

"Priam, your wishes shall be honoured. I shall halt the war for as many days as you ask." Then, taking the old man by the hand, he led him out with Idaeus to their sleeping-place beneath the canvas roof.

Exhausted as they were, they soon drifted off. When all the others were unconscious too, Hermes came again and bent over Priam's pillow.

"Can you sleep among your enemies, old man, and show no fear? Get up and leave this instant, before the other Achaeans learn that you are here."

And so they slipped away into the night. Hermes led them out of the camp until the waters of the Scamander, and from there, alone, carrying the precious remains, they reached the Scaean Gates. It was the hour when rosy-fingered Dawn was spreading her pink veil over the suffering city.

All Troy received dead Hector with displays of grief. His aged parents and beloved wife bathed his divine face with their flowing tears, their longing to weep over his body satisfied at last. Nine days the Trojans brought in wood for Hector's pyre, and when the flames had risen high and burned him they placed his bones inside a golden casket. Next day they buried him outside the wall and raised a tall mound over him. The mighty hero was sent to the next world with the honours he deserved.

Such was the funeral of Hector, and thus Homer brings to an end the immortal epic which we call "The Iliad".

THE LAST DAYS OF TROY

After Hector's death, the Trojans barricaded themselves within their city and did not dare venture out beyond its walls. Yet assistance which they had not hoped for was given them by the warlike Amazons.

Their young queen, Penthesileia, was untried in the arts of battle, and this was not considered fitting for an Amazon ruler. For this reason she decided to come to Troy and fight on Priam's side.

Penthesileia and her women warriors descended suddenly on the Danaid hosts and killed many heroes. Before this irresistible assault the Achaeans fell back far beyond the walls, while Ajax and Achilles were still unaware of what was happening. Grief at the loss of Patroclus kept the son of Peleus confined to his tent, and Ajax, out of sympathy, did not wish to leave him there alone. Eventually the Amazons' pursuit of the Achaeans brought the sound of battle to where the two heroes sat.

At first they did not realise what was going on, but the moment they saw the legendary women driving the fleeing Danaids to their ships, they seized their weapons and hurled themselves upon them. As soon as these two champions entered the fray, the Achaeans regained their lost courage and a savage struggle developed. Shaken by the men's sudden burst of fighting spirit, Penthesileia singled out the one wreaking the worst havoc and launched herself at him. She knew who it was, for Achilles' name had reached the corners of the world by now. Yet far from putting her in fear of him, this only whetted her appetite to pit her skills against his, and so she ran to face him. Three times she charged with her long spear, but three times her thrust was thwarted by Achilles' shield. She made a fourth lunge, but before her blow could reach him, Achilles' fearsome lance caught her full between the ribs – and that was the end of her. The queen of the Amazons sank lifeless to the earth. Wondering at her great valour and daring, hardly believing that this could be a woman who had fought him, the mighty hero lifted the helmet from her face and was so dazzled by her beauty that he was sick at heart for having killed her. Admiringly he kneeled and laid a kiss on her dead lips. He did not take her armour and her weapons, as was the custom in war, but even gave the order that none of the Amazon corpses that lay round her should be touched.

They were all returned, together with their weapons, to be buried by the other Amazons with honours.

After the death of Penthesileia the city gates of Troy were closed once more. Yet not for long, because a brave new ally came to Ilium with a powerful army. This was Memnon the Ethiopian, son of Tithonus and Eos, or rosy-fingered Dawn as the ancients often called her. Memnon's father was a brother of Priam's, and when he heard of the city's plight he sent his son to help the Trojans.

Black as ebony, and of gigantic build, Memnon was a warrior to be trembled at. Some even said his strength was equal to Achilles'. He, too, was born of a goddess and like him he wore armour wrought by Hephaestus.

This son of the Dawn wreaked havoc among the Achaeans. Hero after hero was brought low by his relentless sword, and Achilles had been warned by Thetis that he should not come out to challenge him, for if he killed Memnon then his turn would also come to die. Achilles held to his mother's advice until he learned that Antilochus, the most faithful of his friends since Patroclus' death, had been killed in his turn. This unlucky son of Nestor had died in the most heroic way: stepping in front of his aged father to save him from Memnon's deadly spear, he took the mortal thrust himself. Yet when Antilochus was killed, the manner of his death so grieved and angered Achilles that he disregarded his mother's words of warning and charged impulsively into the fray. He found Memnon in combat with great Ajax, who was struggling to beat off his charges.

"Move aside, Ajax," cried out Achilles, "there are many

others for you to kill. Leave this one to me!"

Achilles was soon locked in deadly struggle with the negro. For the first time in his life he was facing an opponent who could match his strength, and for many hours it was unclear which of the two would emerge victorious from the duel. Both were wounded, Memnon in the shoulder and Achilles in the arm, but they fought on like rabid dogs. Fearful of the outcome, Thetis and Eo each begged Zeus to give the victory to her son.

"Even I cannot erase that which is written," said Zeus and he called on Hermes to weigh the two heroes' fates. The balance swung down heavily against Memnon and with a heart-rending cry his mother hastened to the field of battle. She was too late; Achilles had already dealt her son the fatal blow and Eo was only just in time to bear him up into the heavens and prevent the son of Peleus from stripping him of his armour.

Having killed Memnon, it was now Achilles' turn to die. Flushed with this latest victory, nothing could hold him back, and he hunted the enemy down till they fled behind the Scaean Gates. Such was the fury of his charge that he would have taken Troy single-handed if Apollo had not barred his way. Achilles screamed his rage against the god, threatening even to fell him with his heavy spear; but at this the god grew angrier still, and roared out in a voice that pulsed with wrath:

"Get back, Achilles! Unhappy man, your fate was written from the moment you were born. You shall never enter Troy."

...Achilles sank to his knees. He knew all too well
the meaning of that arrow in his heel...

With these words he hastened to find Paris and ordered him to aim his bow at Achilles from a distance. Catching the arrow in its flight, he turned its course and buried it in the hero's right heel, the only point from which the mighty warrior's soul could leave his body.

Achilles sank to his knees. He knew all too well the meaning of that arrow in his heel – the 'Achilles' heel' as men have called it ever since. Yet he refused to droop into the arms of shadowy death without a struggle. Staggering to his feet, he fell upon the Trojans one last time and killed scores of them as they fled in terror. And when at last death wrapped him in its folds and he felt his powers failing him, he sank to the earth upon one knee and roared a final terrible threat:

"May the gods have mercy on you, Trojans, for I shall be avenged upon you even in death. There is no escape for you!" These were his last words. A moment later the great hero dropped lifeless to the ground. His weapons tumbled with a mighty clash, the earth shook and the heavens clouded over. The most formidable of the combatants, friend or foe, the son of Peleus and Thetis, now lay dead!

A savage struggle immediately broke out around the dead Achilles. The Trojans, led by Aeneas, tried desperately to win his corpse. Ajax and Odysseus made superhuman efforts to defend it. Glaucus, now leader of the Lycians, succeeded in getting a rope tied to the body and began to drag it away. It was a rash attempt and he soon paid for it with his life when Ajax despatched him with his spear. But still the battle raged on, countless dead falling on each side, and neither the Trojans able to drag off the corpse nor the Danaids to beat them back and recover it. One whole day the struggle for the dead Achilles went on, until Zeus, who had witnessed all from the heights of Ida and was filled with pity for him, sent a terrible storm. This put an end to the fighting just long enough for Ajax and Odysseus to bear the body off. Ajax hoisted it upon his burly shoulders while Odysseus covered his retreat. The Trojans pursued them furiously, but thanks to Odysseus' heroic disregard for his own safety and Ajax' tireless strength, the two heroes got Achilles safely back inside the Achaean camp and from there to the ships.

They placed the great hero on a funeral bier and the mourning rites began. All the hosts of the Danaids, with their leaders to the fore, bewailed the noble companion they had lost. The goddess Thetis and her sisters, the fifty daughters of Nereus, came up from the sea and joined their voices in a chant of grief. The nine muses came from Olympus to sing the hymn of the dead over his body. The gods themselves wept at the loss of the Greek champion.

Seventeen days the Achaeans mourned Achilles. On the eighteenth they burned him high on a great pyre together with many beasts they had sacrificed to honour him. Then they took his bones and put them in the same golden urn in which they had placed the ashes of Patroclus. They buried them in the same tomb, which they now made wider and taller, so that it would be seen from a great distance and remind all those who passed up the Hellespont of the glory of the heroes who lay beneath it.

Then funeral games were held in dead Achilles' honour.
The goddess Thetis brought marvellous prizes from beneath the sea and awarded them to the winning athletes to
remind them of the bravery of her son.

Hard on the loss of Achilles, another sad blow fell upon
the Greeks. This was the death of Ajax, son of Telamon.
The hero's end was tragic, for he did not meet a glorious
death in battle but died in the worst way that could happen.
Great Ajax lost his mind and killed himself after being
tricked out of Achilles' splendid weapons, which should
have fallen to him. Since both he and Odysseus had risked
their lives to rescue the body of Thetis' son from the
Trojans, it was decided that lots should be drawn to decide
which of the two should take the fabulous armour wrought
him by Hephaestus. However, Agamemnon and Menelaus
switched the lots around, and while it was Ajax who had
really won, they claimed Odysseus was the winner. The
cheated hero realised what had happened and was seized by
such a paroxysm of rage that he would have killed them
both. Instead, of this he lost his wits and, not knowing what
he did, began to slaughter cattle. Finally, he stuck his sword
point-upwards in the ground and fell on it with all his force.
Even after this frightful death Agamemnon and Menelaus
stubbornly tried to refuse him the burial which was his due.
But Odysseus resisted the sons of Atreus' will with equal
stubbornness till finally Ajax was buried with great honours
and a tomb raised for him at Achilles' side.

Without their two best men, the war became much
harder for the Achaeans. Granted, the Trojans dared not

venture out beyond their walls, yet how was the city to be
taken now, when even with Ajax and Achilles living it had
proved impossible? Calchas told them that his own powers
of prophesy could no longer help, but he added that all the
oracles relating to the fall of Troy were known by Priam's
son Helenus.

From the moment Odysseus heard this, he began to think
of nothing else but how he might capture Helenus to learn
the oracles; and capture him he did, one night when Helenus had slipped out of the city to see what the Achaeans
were preparing.

"There's no escape for you now," Odysseus told him,
"yet there is just one way you can save your skin: tell me
the oracles you know about the fall of Troy."

In his terror, Helenus revealed all.

"There are three oracles relating to the city's end. One
says that Ilium will not be taken without Heracles' arrows,
which are kept by Philoctetes; the second says that Troy
cannot be conquered without the aid of Neoptolemus, the
son of Achilles; and the last says you will never capture
Priam's city unless you first obtain the Palladium, the
statue which is guarded in Athena's temple on the acropolis
of Troy."

Odysseus rushed to tell the other leaders what he had
learned, and offered to see to everything himself. The man
who had once been so reluctant to come and fight at Troy
was now the most determined of all to see this long war end
in victory.

He went first to Scyros, to the palace of king Ly-

comedes, where young Neoptolemus was living. Achilles
had never married, of course; but when he sailed away
from Scyros, where his mother had sent him into hiding, he
had left Deidameia, Lycomedes' daughter, weeping bitter
tears. In her womb there stirred the fruit of her love for
Achilles, a secret shared by the two of them alone. Many
years had passed since then. The first, unsuccessful
Achaean expedition had returned, eight more years had
passed before the armies reassembled, and the war itself
had lasted another ten years. Achilles' son Neoptolemus
was now a fine sturdy young man filled with a love of
battle and a yearning for great deeds. Odysseus had no
difficulty in persuading Lycomedes to hand him over and
Neoptolemus was eager to depart.

Accompanied by Achilles' son, Odysseus next sailed for
Lemnos, where the Achaeans had deserted Philoctetes all
those years before. It was not easy for Odysseus to persuade that suffering hero to come with them, for he had
nursed a hatred for him and all the leaders of the Danaids,
ever since the snake had bitten him and they had abandoned
him on Lemnos to suffer years of pain. He was finally
convinced by Heracles himself, who had joined the immortals on Olympus and now advised him to go to Troy, for
there his wound would heal at last and he would find great
glory.

And so Odysseus returned to Ilium, with Philoctetes
bearing Heracles' arrows, and young Neoptolemus, to
whom he willingly relinquished his father Achilles' weapons.

From the very start, the two new arrivals rendered the Achaeans services of inestimable value.

As soon as he arrived in camp, Philoctetes was cured by the wise healer, Machaon, and immediately demanded to face Paris in single combat. That foolish man hastened to accept the challenge, not knowing that Philoctetes possessed Heracles' arrows which were steeped in the poisonous blood of the Lernaean Hydra.

Three arrows were loosed by Paris and three by Philoctetes. Paris' shots all missed; of Philoctetes' arrows, the first failed to find its target, the second struck Paris' bow close to the handgrip and the third caught him on the ankle. That was enough. The poison of the Lernaean Hydra entered Paris' bloodstream.

The instant Paris was wounded, he let out a howl of pain and hobbled out of range. The Trojans immediately carried him back off to the city, but his condition quickly worsened and Paris realised that his end was near.

It was then that he remembered Oenone, his first love. "If ever you are wounded," she had said, "then come to me – for I alone can cure your ills." And so he asked to be carried to the mountain where the lovely nymph had her home. But this man whom all had grown to hate was now loathed even by the nymph who had once loved him so desperately. She refused to heal his wound, and so, despairing, he returned to die in Troy. Soon regretting her hardheartedness, Oenone followed after him. By the time she reached him, though, it was too late. Paris was dead.

After his death, Helenus and Deiphobus quarrelled as to

who would take fair Helen as his wife. Deiphobus won, but Helen now remembered Menelaus and the daughter she had left in Sparta and did not wish to marry yet again. She tried to escape down a rope thrown over the walls, but she was caught and brought back to Deiphobus, who married her despite her violent protests.

If Philoctetes won instant glory by his slaying Paris, Neoptolemus, too, was to win rapid fame by fighting the mighty hero Eurypylus, the newest of Priam's allies. Eurypylus, who was not only the latest but the last of those who would bring aid to Troy, was son of king Telephus of Mysia. Like his father, Eurypylus, was a fearless warrior and killed many of the Achaean heroes.

Among them was the gifted healer Machaon, the son of Asclepius. From then on, at the temple of Asclepius in Mysia, although the memory of Telephus continued to be held in reverence, the name of his brave son was never mentioned after he had killed Asclepius' famous son. Much as he helped the Trojans, Eurypylus could not withstand the furious charges of Neoptolemus in the end and lost his life and weapons alike. After the slaying of Eurypylus the Trojans were forced to barricade themselves behind their walls once more – and they were never again to emerge.

In the meantime, Odysseus had been giving constant thought to Helenus' last oracle, the Palladium. Finally he decided to enter Troy alone and steal it. First dressing like a beggar, he then told Diomedes to whip him till his whole body was a mass of bloody weals, and in this sorry state he entered Troy and pleaded for protection. All pitied him on hearing the lying tales he told of the tortures he had suffered when he fell into Achaean hands, and how he had escaped them. Everyone believed him, until his stories reached fair Helen's ears. Her sharp mind told her to beware of this man, for his voice and his persuasive words reminded her immediately of Odysseus. She put certain questions to him, and he, knowing full well why she did so, used every ounce of skill that he possessed to dispel all her suspicions. Then Helen thought of a clever ruse: pretending that she pitied him, she persuaded the Trojans to let her take this poor, whipped beggar to the palace and have him tended. Once there, she made him bathe to wash off all the dirt and blood, then gave him clean clothes to put on. When he appeared before her, not only did she recognize Odysseus at once but he, too, could keep up the pretence no longer.

"Do not be afraid, though," she reassured him, "I am held here like a slave now and have no reason to betray you. As far as I'm concerned, you're free to do whatever you were planning — and I will even help you if you want."

Odysseus, however, preferred to work alone on secret missions, and putting on his beggar's rags he slipped out unobserved in the middle of the night. He went first to the temple of Athena. He stole the Palladium without any difficulty, for the goddess herself put the guards to sleep. Then he went down into the city. When he reached the Scaean Gates he gave battle single-handed with the whole company that guarded them. The invisible Athena helped him to kill the greater number, while the remainder, demoralised and all too grateful to have cheated death, opened the gates for him with their own hands. Thus Odysseus carried off the Palladium beyond the walls, sealing the Trojans' fate.

It did not take Odysseus long to work out the actual means by which Troy might be taken. It was Athena who slipped the idea of the Wooden Horse into his mind. In its huge belly a whole troop of warriors could be hidden. Somehow, though, the Trojans would have to be deceived into dragging the horse within the city walls of their own free will. It was a bold concept, but all went as planned.

The task of building the horse was undertaken by Epeius. Although this leader had brought thirty ships with him to Troy, he was the most cowardly of all the Achaeans. He had not taken part in a single battle and his only contribution to the fighting was to bring water to Agamemnon and Menelaus. Yet now the hour of glory had come even for this most timid of men. And it was his due – for Epeius was blessed with such skilled hands that nothing was beyond his capabilities. Ordering a whole mountainside of tree-trunks to be brought to him, he set to work with a will. In a few days the marvellous Wooden Horse was ready, perfect in every detail and exactly as Odysseus had wanted it. That night they trundled it up close to the walls and forty chosen warriors climbed into its belly with their weapons. Among them were all the Achaeans' best-known leaders, except for Agamemnon, who would have to remain with the army. The last to get inside the horse was the terror-stricken Epeius, who was needed because only he knew the way to open and close the hidden door. The same night, on Odysseus' instructions, Agamemnon ordered the Greek camp to be burned, and with all the troops on board the fleet set sail for Tenedos, the little island off the coast of Troy, where it would stand ready to return the moment the signal light was given.

This message would be flashed with a burning torch by Sinon, the only man who had remained in the deserted camp. But this would not be Sinon's only task. The wily Odysseus had rehearsed with him exactly how he was to let himself fall into Trojan hands and then continue to deceive them lest they smash or burn the Wooden Horse. Since Sinon was Odysseus' cousin and, like him, well-known for his crafty ways, a better man could not have been chosen for the job.

When dawn began to flood the heavens with her pearly light, the Trojans on the walls were struck with awe by what they saw. They sent a messenger running to fetch Priam, who hastened to the tower above the Scaean Gates and could not believe his eyes when he looked down. From the enemy's deserted camp thick clouds of smoke still rose, and not far from the city walls an enormous wooden horse was standing. Priam ordered the great gates to be opened and came out surrounded by a crowd of nobles. They approached the horse in awe and curiosity. On it was an inscription: "A gift from the Achaeans to Athena, whom they beseech to help them reach their homeland speedily."

They were all deeply impressed and one of them suggested:

"Since it is an offering to Athena, let us bring it into the city and carry it up the acropolis to watch over us."

"No!" shouted another. "Since Athena is with the Achaeans we must burn it on the spot – or better still break it open to see if there is anything hidden inside."

"Woe betide us if we mistreat that which belongs to the great goddess," Priam warned. "If we want Athena to come over to our side, there is no doubt we must drag it into the city."

"We should neither destroy it nor let it come within the city walls," advised far-seeing Antenor. "Even if we leave it here we can dedicate it to the goddess and offer her rich sacrifices."

While various opinions were being offered, a prisoner was dragged in with kicks and curses. Of course, it was none other than Sinon, who had surrendered to some shepherds.

"Tell us who you are," Priam commanded, "and why you did not leave together with the others."

With a perfectly convincing air, Sinon unfolded the tale which he had learned by heart:

"The accursed Odysseus hated me and longed to have me killed, since I was the only one who knew the secret of Palamedes' death. He convinced the others that someone must be sacrificed to the gods to make the wind blow and carry us back home – and he chose me. But at the fatal moment a wind rose of its own accord. In the haste and bustle of the preparations for departure, I managed to escape."

Hearing these words, Priam took pity on him; and, worse
still for himself and all of Troy, he asked with naive trust:

"Tell me, now, why did the Achaeans build this wooden
horse?"

Sinon had only been waiting on this question to launch
into the second chapter of the fairytale Odysseus had taught
him.

"We made this horse to placate Athena, who was angry
with us because Odysseus stole the Palladium. Three times
flames shot from the statue, and we were filled with fear.
Then Calchas told us Troy would never be taken now
because we had lost Athena's support, and that the only
course left to us was to go back to our homes. And so the
goddess would not give us a rough journey, he advised us
to build the horse as an offering to her."

"And why so large?" asked Priam.

Sinon had been expecting this question, too; and once
more he had the answer ready:

"So that you could not bring it into the city," he replied;
"for if this horse, a gift to Athena, should ever pass within
your walls you would become so strong that you could
conquer golden Mycenae and hold sway over all Greece.
Yet if you destroy it, Troy, too, will be destroyed."

So convincing was Sinon that not only Priam but all his
nobles, too, were persuaded that the Wooden Horse must
be dragged inside the walls and raised high on the acropolis.

And that is what they did. The horse was so huge,
though, that they had to demolish a section of the walls to

do so. Even then it was a struggle to heave it through the gap, and four times the horse jarred against the sides of the opening with a loud clash from the weapons of the warriors inside. But Athena closed the Trojans' ears to the suspicious noise and they struggled upwards with their burden till at last it was mounted high on the acropolis before the temple of the goddess. Yet the moment Laocoön, the great soothsayer and brother of Anchises, saw it there he cried:

"What are you doing, Trojans? Have you still not learned of the cunning of Odysseus? Do you believe the enemy has left for home? That horse is filled with Achae-

ans armed to the teeth. Mark my words: 'Beware the Danaids, even when they bring gifts!'" So saying, he plunged his spear into the belly of the wooden horse. The violence of the impact shook its frame, rattling the weapons of the Greeks who were inside.

"Burn it!" came a chorus of frightened voices.

"Heave it off the city walls!" cried others.

The warriors in the horse's belly were seized with fear. Between his sobs, the timid Epeius cursed the day he had ever built the thing. Only Neoptolemus was undismayed, and he urged Odysseus that they should leave their hiding-place at once and throw themselves upon the Trojans. But Odysseus refused to be drawn by this display of youthful zeal and held firmly to his plan, which was to climb out of the horse unnoticed under the cover of darkness. As for their present danger, this was soon surpassed when they heard Priam shout that he would allow no one to harm the Wooden Horse. Yet even then the Trojans were not pacified until news came that two huge serpents had slithered out of the sea and attacked Laocoön's two sons as they were sacrificing to Apollo. Their father ran to save them, but in vain. All three fell victim to the serpents' poisonous fangs. Now it was clear to all: Laocoön had been punished for his irreverence in daring to strike with his spear the horse which was dedicated to Athena. There could be no further doubt – the war was over and the enemy had gone. What if the Palladium was lost, when now the Trojans had the Wooden Horse to protect their city for all time?

But then Cassandra came running towards them, shouting:

"What are you doing, fools? That horse will bring destruction on us! Burn it, if you wish Troy to be saved!"

Alas, who would listen to Cassandra's prophetic words when she was fated never to be believed!"

With feasting and dancing, the victory celebrations began. The whole city was decked with flowers, and a carpet of rose-petals was strewn at the feet of the Wooden Horse. All were wild with joy and only Cassandra cried repeatedly: "What are you doing, fools? The moment of Troy's destruction is upon us!" Yet the merry-makers' only reac-

...Now it was clear to all: Laocoön had been punished for his irreverence in daring to strike with his spear the horse...

tion was pity for her, that she would not celebrate the ending of this fearsome war along with them.

All day the Trojans rejoiced, and when night fell they were so overcome by their feasting and deep drinking that they fell into a heavy sleep. Not a man among them was alert and on his feet. Even Cassandra's voice had finally failed her after so many hours of vain warnings.

At last, when silence shrouded the whole city, Sinon slipped through the gap in the wall and ran to the tomb of Achilles. Climbing to the top of the mound with a flaming torch held high above his head, he gave the signal which had been agreed to the Achaeans waiting opposite on Tenedos. Agamemnon answered with another burning brand and the fleet set sail at once. It was not long before the ships had reached the Trojan shores, where the troops all disembarked and advanced silently upon the city. At the same moment, Odysseus ordered Epeius to open the secret door in the horse's underbelly. Sliding on ropes, they descended one by one in the bright moonlight. On tiptoe, the well-armed heroes crept down to the city. Utter silence reigned; not even a dog barked. They reached the walls, where the tired and drunken guards were fast asleep like all the others – a sleep from which they never woke again, for the Achaeans slew them and opened wide the gates. The forces of Agamemnon were already outside, Now there was nothing to hold them back, and they surged in from the gates and the breached wall to begin their terrible work. Like ravening lions that fall upon a slumbering flock at night, so the Acheans fell upon the unsuspecting city, whose sleeping calm was shattered. Before they could even reach for their weapons, countless brave Trojans were slaughtered within instants. Groans echoed through the streets. The air was rent by the shrieks of women and the terrified wails of children. As many Trojans as had time leapt to their feet, armed themselves with whatever weapons came to hand, even the spits on which a few short hours before they had been roasting lambs, and went out to give battle. But the odds were all against them, and soon the place was filled with lifeless bodies and its roads were drowned in rivers of its children's blood. That terrible night, Troy writhed in its death-throes.

Neoptolemus raced for the palace, accompanied by Odysseus and Menelaus. They smashed down the doors, and old Priam, unable to resist, took refuge in the sanctuary of Zeus. But to no avail. Neoptolemus seized him and respecting neither his grey hairs nor his rank he slew him on the palace staircase. Meanwhile, Menelaus was running through the corridors in search of Helen's room. Outside her door he found Deiphobus, her current husband. His blood boiled at the sight of him.

"Miserable cur!" he roared, "Now you will pay for everything, for that 'death to the foreigners' you shouted out when we came to ask that our quarrel be resolved by peaceful means, and for your insolence in marrying this faithless woman when you could not see, blind fool, that the days of Troy were numbered on the fingers of one hand!"

Deiphobus could find no other answer but to hurl his

spear. In vain, however, and his end came swiftly. Sword in hand, Menelaus threw himself upon his enemy and struck him lifeless to the ground.

The son of Atreus had no time to waste. Stepping over the body, he rushed towards the inner rooms to complete his task, for he had sworn he would kill Helen, too. Soon he stood before her. Twenty years had passed since she betrayed him, and ten of those years had been filled with bloodshed and grim horror. All because of her. Raising his sword, he prepared to slay her. But Helen was sorry for all her misdeeds and her abiding love for Menelaus told her what it was she must do now.

"Kill me," she said, baring her breast, "for I am guilty."

And then Menelaus recalled his wife as she had once been, long before, before Aphrodite had turned her head, and he put his sword back in its sheath. Without a word, he caught her by the hand and led her to the ships.

Meanwhile, the terrible slaughter continued in the city. All the sons of Priam were killed, and all the brave men of Troy, while their wives and lovely daughters were dragged down to the Achaean ships as slaves. Among them were Hecabe, Cassandra and Andromache. In vain did they cry out for rescue, for not one of their family or friends was left alive to hear them and be moved by their pleas.

Little Astyanax, Hector's baby son, was not spared either. The Achaeans were determined that no descendant of Priam should be left alive, so there would be no one who could ever seek revenge.

Ajax of Locris behaved most vilely towards Cassandra,

who had sought protection from the gods inside the temple of Athena. The unlucky soothsayer was clinging to the statue of the goddess, but Ajax tore her from it with such force that the holy image was toppled from its base and smashed to pieces on the floor. Worst of all, he then assaulted Cassandra within the holy precinct. A thousand years the Locrids would pay for Ajax' hideous sacrilege.

After the slaughter, the looting of the city started. The Achaeans seized whatever they could lay their hands on, then hauled it down to the waiting ships. Priam's palace was stripped of everything precious it contained – and when there was nothing left to sack, the work of destruction was finished by the torch. Flames shot heavenward and engulfed the whole of Troy, transforming it to ashes and blackened ruins. Nothing would remain of noble Hector's city but a bitter memory. The long history of Troy closes on this tragic note, with Hera and Athena obtaining the vengeance they had sought – and a thousand pities for it.

However heartlessly the victors may have dealt with the luckless Trojans, there were two cases in which they showed themselves both fair and sympathetic.

They did not harm the just Antenor and the four of his sons who had not been killed in previous battles. One of these was saved by Odysseus himself, when the Achaeans were about to cut him down. And Menelaus even offered Antenor a ship so that he could sail away with his family and the Venicians, a small band of foot-soldiers he had brought to Troy from the city of that name in Paphlagonia. Antenor set course westwards and eventually made landfall at the head of the Adriatic sea, where he built a city which he named New Troy and which is known to us today as Venice.

The other example of humane treatment was that shown to Aeneas.

Carrying his blind father on his back and holding his young son by the hand, Aeneas left Troy by the Dardanian Gates. The enemy was around him, behind him and before him and he walked on bent low, looking only at the ground beneath his feet. If the Achaeans were to fall on them, he knew that there was no escape.

"Who are you letting get away? That is Aeneas!" shouted somebody, and drawing his sword he ran to strike him down, only to be stopped by a voice from close at hand crying out: "Shame on you!" It was Diomedes who had spoken, he who had been Aeneas' most deadly opponent in the hour of battle. Thus Anchises' son passed with his precious cargo through the armed ranks of the Greeks, who not only let him go unharmed, but stood aside to make way for him.

Aeneas pursued his way towards mount Ida. Behind him, Ilium burned, and with it all that lay around. Home-land he no longer had – and so but one solution remained: to find another. With a few companions he boarded a ship and like Antenor set sail towards the west. After a long and adventure-filled voyage he at last reached central Italy and there, on the bank of the river Tiber, he built a city which he named Lavinium. On the same river, a little further from the sea, Rome, the capital of an empire which was to rule

...Carrying his blind father on his back and holding his
young son by the hand, Aeneas left Troy...

the world, was later built. Its citizens recalled with pride that the founder of their race was Aeneas, the son of Aphrodite.

After they had looted and burned Troy the Achaeans boarded their ships and set sail for Greece, eager to see their homeland once again. With them they carried an immense treasure and all the able-bodied women and children of the Trojans, who were now their slaves. There was no question of taking men as well. None of them had escaped the blood-bath – and besides, a brave warrior never makes a good slave.

For most of the leaders the voyage homewards proved no easy undertaking, and only old Nestor, Diomedes and two or three others arrived without delay and with all their ships intact.

Ajax of Locris, who had treated Cassandra in such a bestial fashion, never reached home at all. To punish him, Athena drove his ships upon the rugged coast of Euboea, and in one terrible night they were all smashed on the rocky shore.

Agamemnon, too, was wrecked in the same spot; but although the wild waves did not drag him down, death was waiting for him in Mycenae at the hands of Aegisthus with a weapon provided by none other than his own wife Clytemnestra – and she it was who killed the unfortunate Cassandra, whom Agamemnon had brought back with him as a slave.

Neither did Menelaus have an uneventful voyage home to Sparta. He incurred the wrath of the goddess Athena by his disrespectful remark that the Achaeans owed her nothing since it had taken them ten years to conquer Troy. As a result, he and Helen suffered hardships in distant lands for eight whole years; but when at last they did reach Sparta, they lived out the rest of their days together. And when they died, almighty Zeus did not let Charon carry them off to the dark kingdom of Hades, but sent Hermes to lead them to the Elysian fields, where Menelaus and the fair Helen have lived ever since without further pain or sorrow.

Yet of all those who had set out to take Troy, none had a harder or a longer journey home than did Odysseus. Unwittingly, he made an enemy of the great god of the sea, earth-shaker Poseidon. As a result he was driven here and there upon the face of the waters for ten whole years, and did not make his way back to Ithaca until he had lost all his ships and every one of his companions. The sufferings, the wanderings and the deeds of this wiliest of heroes have all been set down for us by the great poet Homer in another epic, the splendid 'Odyssey', and these we shall tell of in our next volume.

THE AUTHOR OF THE ILIAD AND THE ODYSSEY

The Trojan War, which scholars tell us must have taken place around 1200 B.C., marks the end of an epoch. Indeed, within a space of not more than a hundred years, Mycenaean civilization disappeared and a dark age fell on Greece which lasted between two and three centuries. Yet although all else was shrouded in the blanket of the dark, the cultural legacy of the world that had been lost shone through and lived on to become the seed of that brilliant flowering of the Hellenic spirit which was yet to come. What was saved we now call Greek Mythology. Handed down by word of mouth, from one singer to another, around seven hundred years before the birth of Christ it reached the ears of Homer, and from the rich store he had at his disposal he crafted his two immortal epics, the 'Iliad' and the 'Odyssey'. Although these works have come down to us mutilated and 'improved', they still overflow with the inspired words of a giant of poetry, yet one of whom tradition has nothing certain to tell us but his name. But what difference does it make whether Homer was born in Smyrna, on Chios or in Argos, and whether he was blind or not, when we can come to know him through his work, that mirror of his soul?

Homer was a genius whom critics past and present alike have placed at the very summit of the pyramid, alone or

accompanied by two or three great names from world
literature at most. It is not sufficient for a work of literature
to move us by its poetic qualities alone. It must move us,
too, by the truth with which it reflects our human condition.
Homer excels in both. The poetry of his language often
rises to heights of incomparable beauty, as in the parting of
Hector from Andromache, or the scene at the end of the
'Iliad' in which Priam asks Achilles for the body of his son.
What universal human values are enshrined in this parting!
And how can Achilles, who, by dragging Hector's body in
the dust, has outraged even the gods who love him, now
receive king Priam in his tent? How could he find room for
so much sympathy in a heart so filled with bitter rage? Can
a man at times be hard and savage and at others kind and
yielding? The truth is that he can. This is what our poet told
us three thousand years ago, and he is right. But that is
Homer for you: measured, decent and above all unbiassed.
While he proclaims that 'there is nothing sweeter in the
world than motherland and parents', his vision of humanity
is so universal as to have an Achaean and a Trojan embrace
in death. Not for him the good on one side and the evil on
the other, but only men ranged in battle against their fellow
men. Homer loves his country, but he also loves mankind
beyond all national boundaries, and there is no contradic-
tion in this. He loves his homeland and his people best who
has the deepest springs of love in him. Many men have
been great but not all have been true of heart. Homer was
both.